The Local
INTER FAITH
GUIDE

Faith Community Co-operation in Action

government and other public bodies in the valuable role which local inter faith organisations can play.

Thanks are due to all who helped with this publication, including the Executive Committee and member bodies of the Inter Faith Network, the Secretariat and Council members of the Inner Cities Religious Council and the Cohesion and Faiths Unit of the Home Office. Thank you also to local groups which contributed or cleared case study materials and to the University of Derby which has allowed us to draw, for some sections of the present publication, on previous work done jointly with them for the publication *Religions in the UK: A Directory 2001-03* and to Sandy Adirondack, consultant on voluntary sector governance, for her comments on sections of the text relating to organisational matters.

We are also grateful to the Inter Faith Network's staff and, in particular, to Harriet Crabtree for her work on writing and researching the guide.

We are particularly grateful to those who have supported this project, including the Office of the Deputy Prime Minister and the Church Urban Fund.

RT REVD DR TOM BUTLER   JAGJIWAN SINGH

Table of Contents

1 | Introduction

The scope and focus of the guide

There are many different ways to get involved in building good relations between people of different faiths. This guide looks at one very important type of initiative: local inter faith organisations. These encourage co-operation, encounter, understanding and respect between members of the different faith communities in the UK at grassroots level.

Although many of the ideas in the guide are relevant to national or regional inter faith bodies, the guide's focus is on the local: on initiatives ranging from town or city to county level (but with local grassroots involvement) in scope.

The guide concentrates on initiatives which bridge all the main faith communities in an area and which address issues of mutual interest and concern to them. These multilateral links are of particular importance in addressing the 'civic' agenda, including such issues as the kinds of facilities and services needed to provide appropriately for people of different faiths.

There are also important initiatives which promote dialogue and understanding between two, or three, particular traditions. Sometimes refered to as 'bilateral' or 'trilateral' initiatives, these have a very valuable role in furthering inter faith understanding. They enable particularly deep discussion of the shared histories and concerns of the traditions in question, which is required if past distrust and even hostility are to be overcome. It is not possible in the scope of this brief guide to explore these initiatives in depth, but their work is covered in greater detail in *Inter Faith Organisations in the UK: A Directory* (see under Resources: Publications). Most are branches of national bodies such as the Council of Christians and Jews and the Three Faiths Forum.

The guide has particularly in mind readers living in multi faith towns and cities although there are, of course, many areas of the

UK where religious diversity is limited, but where people are keen to develop greater inter faith awareness and understanding. Inter faith initiatives in these areas have a signficant role in encouraging a better understanding across the UK as a whole of the issues which need to be addressed in our more religiously diverse society. Similarly, although the guide refers primarily to people of various faiths, valuable contributions may be made to understanding about religious issues by individuals who have no formal faith affiliation but value the spiritual dimension in their lives.

The focus of the present guide is on issues related to 'religious identity' rather than 'ethnic identity'. Sometimes there is significant overlap between these aspects of identity, but most of Britain's faith communities have members of varied ethnic backgrounds. In the inter faith context, religious or faith identity is the significant factor, although of course building good inter faith relations makes an important contribution to community relations more generally.

In this guide you will find basic information about setting up local inter faith bodies and about strengthening the work of existing ones. This draws on the experience of the Inter Faith Network office and of local inter faith bodies which participated in a major survey of local inter faith activity carried out by Network, with support from the Home Office, in 2003 and in a follow up information gathering exercise which enabled the Network to create a directory of inter faith organisations around the UK[1]. For the present guide, many new case studies have been gathered.[2]

A note about government engagement with inter faith issues

This new edition of the guide is published in association with the Inner Cities Religious Council of the Office of the Deputy Prime Minister (ODPM). It takes account of the work in which the Network has been involved in the last few years with the Local Government Association, the Office of the Deputy Prime Minister and the Home Office in promoting a clearer picture of the fruitful relationship which can be established between local authorities, other public agencies and faith communities in their areas; the encouragement which local authorities can give to local inter faith initiatives; and the contribution of these approaches to the wider community cohesion agenda.[3]

The ODPM, in partnership with the Home Office and Government Offices for the Regions, is currently developing a link between local authority officials with responsibility for faith and inter faith issues based mainly on those local authority areas in England with the highest levels of diversity according to the 2001 census statistics on religious identity. This will enable them to keep in touch with developments on engaging with faith communities and inter faith bodies at local level.

Further resources

The section Resources: Organisations at the back of the guide contains information on the Inter Faith Network, the Inner Cities Religious Council and a range of other organisations which can be of help to local inter faith organisations in various ways. The Network's website, www.interfaith.org.uk, provides contact details for many local inter faith groups around the UK and also links to the websites of national inter faith bodies and faith community representative bodies.

The Inter Faith Network can help with requests for information and advice from those involved in local inter faith activity. The Network also arranges meetings where the organisers of local inter faith initiatives can exchange news and ideas and discuss topics of shared concern and interest.

In Scotland local inter faith bodies will find it particularly helpful to be in touch with the Scottish Inter Faith Council which holds regular meetings for local inter faith organisers. In Northern Ireland, the Northern Ireland Inter Faith Forum can offer direct assistance to any new local bodies. The recently developed Inter Faith Council for Wales may, in the future, offer a similar resource for inter faith bodies in Wales. Contact details for these bodies can be found in the Resources section.

The major faith communities in the UK are all developing programmes of work which contribute to building good inter faith relations in the UK. Some, such as the Churches, have staff with a dedicated inter faith brief. Others, such as the Muslim Council of Britain, have committees looking after this area of work. National faith community bodies are therefore particularly important resources for local inter faith bodies which are seeking information on such issues as the approach to inter faith issues of the different faiths or are wanting to find faith speakers for special events. Contact details for these bodies are listed at the back of the guide.

Keeping in touch

We hope this present guide's suggestions may be helpful in the important inter faith work which you and others are undertaking. We look forward to being kept in touch with initiatives and how they are developing.

1 *Local Inter Faith Activity in the UK: A Survey*, Inter Faith Network for the UK, 2003.

  Inter Faith Organisations in the UK: A Directory, Second Edition, Inter Faith Network for the UK, 2005.

2 The case studies in this guide have been chosen to illustrate particular themes and topics. They do not reflect the overall activities of featured groups.

3 *Faith and Community: A Good Practice Guide for Local Authorities*, Local Government Association in association with the Inner Cities Religious Council of the Office of the Deputy Prime Minister, Active Community Unit of the Home Office, and Inter Faith Network, 2002.

  Guidance on Community Cohesion, Local Government Association in association with the Home Office, Office of the Deputy Prime Minister, Commission for Racial Equality and Inter Faith Network, 2002.

  Partnership for the Common Good: Inter Faith Structures and Local Government, Inter Faith Network in association with the Home Office, Office of the Deputy Prime Minister and Local Government Association, 2003.

  Community Cohesion: An Action Guide, Local Government Association in partnership with the Home Office, Office of the Deputy Prime Minister, Audit Commission, Commission for Racial Equality, Improvement and Development Agency, and Inter Faith Network, 2004.

2 | Local inter faith initiatives

In the 2001 Census, 76.8% of people in the United Kingdom identified themselves as having a religious faith.[1] Even in areas not considered as particularly 'multi faith' or 'multi cultural', there are adherents of most major faiths. In an increasingly diverse UK building good inter faith relations becomes ever more important and in the last few years there has been a steep increase in local initiatives to bring people of different faiths together. The following chart shows just how substantial the increase in local inter faith bodies in the last thirty years has been, particularly since 2001.[2]

Local inter faith bodies

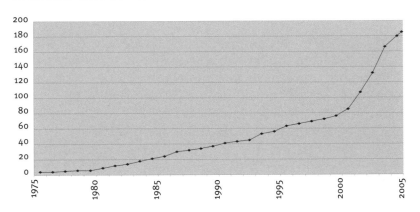

Types of local inter faith organisations

Local inter faith organisations are of many kinds. For example:

Inter faith groups and associations where a group of people of different faiths meet to learn about their respective faiths and discuss issues of common interest. These tend be open to all comers and to have discussion and special events as their focus. Some are relatively informal whereas others opt to plan a programme of meetings for the year, have a simple constitution and charge a small membership fee to cover postage of the year's programme. The formalisation process is often linked to a group taking on a more public role, including, for example, raising the public's awareness of the importance of religious identity or giving advice on religious issues to the local authority.

Councils or forums bringing faith groups together on a broadly representative basis are initiatives which have been structured to include members of each major faith represented in the area. The constitution is usually designed to ensure this participation. They tend to involve the leadership of the local faith communities (as well as other faith community members). Such councils usually have a programme of events to deepen inter faith understanding and cooperation but, because of their representative nature, can also be used as policy sounding boards by outside bodies such as local government.

Multi faith forums and partnerships and faith networks. These are usually set up by, or with the assistance of, local authorities or Local Strategic Partnerships to create a mechanism for nominating to the Local Strategic Partnership and giving input to this and to other initiatives. Some have a significant role in regeneration or neighourhood renewal. Often multi faith partnerships also act as a forum for inter faith discussion between local faith groups and this is what makes them also 'inter faith initiatives'.[3]

There is no fixed pattern and no 'correct' model. What matters is developing an inter faith initiative which meets what are seen as the main local needs.

Perhaps one of the major achievements of **Oldham Inter Faith Forum** since its inception has simply been a readiness and a commitment, on the part of the leaders of the different faiths represented in Oldham, to work jointly to foster mutual understanding. The fact that we have assembled together on a regular basis, prayed together, worked together, eaten together and properly constituted ourselves as a legal entity has eloquently proclaimed the message of cohesion.

Different motivations for setting up local inter faith organisations

There are many different and valid reasons for setting up a local inter faith organisation, for example to:

● ensure that key figures in each faith community come to know each other and develop relationships of mutual trust and support and to encourage friendships across traditions at all levels

● enable members of different faiths to come together to work to improve local civic life and, indeed, be part of a UK-wide movement toward inter religious co-operation with integrity on matters of common concern

● learn about others' faith traditions and help one's own be understood better

● undertake joint projects

● contribute to a cohesive and harmonious local community

● help tackle prejudice and lessen the likelihood of inter religious discord

It is important to be aware that not everyone's understanding of the inter faith process is the same. Members of different faiths are likely to have different understandings, rooted in the teaching of their own particular traditions, about why working for inter faith understanding is important. A person who believes strongly in the uniqueness of their tradition will not respond positively to being told that "all religions are really one and the same". Conversely, someone who sees commonality as more significant than difference will not share the basic assumptions of the person who emphasises the separate, distinct nature of their own and other faith traditions. Motivations and attitudes to inter faith encounter can differ, but where there is goodwill there can be openness to work constructively even where beliefs are not shared.

In recent years, local authorities have shown increased interest in helping set up or support local inter faith structures. The Local Government Association's *Community Cohesion: An Action Guide* notes that "harmonious co-existence of people of different faiths and beliefs is vital to community cohesion" and says that "local authorities should actively encourage projects which increase inter faith understanding and cooperation."[4] A practical step for local authorities is to "establish and sustain a strong local inter faith structure for inter faith cooperation and a mechanism for consultation with faith communities or support an existing forum."

In 2003, a good practice booklet for local authorities, *Partnership for the Common Good: Inter Faith Structures and Local Government*, was published by the Inter Faith Network with the LGA, the Home Office and the Office of the Deputy Prime Minister. This looks at the reasons local authorities and Local Strategic Partnerships have an interest in this area and at factors they may wish to consider if they are planning work involving inter faith or multi faith consultation. It will be of value particularly to readers from such bodies.[5]

1 See www.statistics.gov.uk where the census statistics can be found, as can a useful document, *Focus on Religion*, which draws on these statistics to give socio-economic profiles of the different faiths in the UK. This was published by the Office for National Statistics in 2004.

2 The chart reflects the number of independent local inter faith bodies. The data was gathered for *Local Inter Faith Activity in the UK: A Survey*, Inter Faith Network, 2003 and updated during research for *Inter Faith Organisations in the UK: A Directory*, Second Edition, Inter Faith Network, 2005.

3 See also p 31 of the current Guide on the choice to use the term 'multi faith' rather than 'inter faith'.

4 *Community Cohesion: An Action Guide*, Local Government Association in partnership with the Audit Commission, Commission for Racial Equality, Home Office, Improvement & Development Agency, Inter Faith Network and Office of the Deputy Prime Minister, 2004, pp 29-30.

5 *Partnership for the Common Good: Inter Faith Structures and Local Government*, Inter Faith Network in association with the Home office, Office of the Deputy Prime Minister and Local Government Association, 2003.

3 | Getting involved in local inter faith activity

Join an existing local inter faith organisation

The main way to get involved in building good relations between people of different faiths locally is through an inter faith body. To find out if there is one in your area, look in *Inter Faith Organisations in the UK: A Directory* (see under Resources: Publications) or at the list of local groups on the Inter Faith Network's website www.interfaith.org.uk

If you do not find a local inter faith body listed for your area, check with your own place of worship or with the local Council for Voluntary Service, local authority and library to see if one has recently come into existence or is being planned.

Starting a new local inter faith initiative

The chances are that there is already a local inter faith body in your area. If not, you may think that one should be developed. Chapter 4 gives some pointers for starting a new local inter faith initiative.

You may also want to develop a new initiative if there is an existing initiative but this does not see itself as covering all the areas or inter faith functions that would be desirable. There are a number of areas where there are two or even three overlapping and somewhat different local inter faith bodies. Each fulfils a different function. Where this is the case, complementary working is very important.

4 | Starting a new initiative

If you are thinking of working on a new local inter faith initiative for your area some questions it is helpful to ask at an early stage are:

a) What kind of inter faith initiative might be best for our area?
b) Are we aiming to be 'representative' of local faith communities?
c) What area should our inter faith initiative cover?
d) Who do we need to consult first?
e) How shall we make the initial links?
f) Which local faith organisations need to be on board at the outset to ensure that the initiative is well backed and high profile?
g) Who will make the project their top priority?

Local authority and Local Strategic Partnership readers should note that *Partnership for the Common Good: Inter Faith Structures and Local Government* (see under Resources: Publications) looks at some of these issues particularly from their perspective.

a) What kind of inter faith initiative might be best for our area?

There may be a variety of different views on what sort of inter faith initiative would be of greatest benefit to a particular locality. Some of the types of local inter faith body are outlined in Chapter 2. There is no hard and fast rule for what is most appropriate.

Although representative faith forums and councils are often what is needed in multi faith areas, informal groups with a special focus on religious and spiritual issues continue to play a valuable role and often allow discussion at much greater depth. They can be very rewarding for those who take part in them and help to promote good inter faith relations at the personal level of friendship.

b) Are we aiming to be 'representative' of local faith communities?

You may feel that a representative council is what your area needs, but find the idea of actually getting one going rather daunting! It is true that it involves quite a lot of work but the benefits to the wider community can be considerable. It may be that a perfect pattern of representation cannot be achieved, but there is value in setting the goal of reflecting in membership and management the major faith communities of the area.[1] It is in this sense that the present guide calls it a 'representative' council, not necessarily in terms of each attender being a formally elected representative, even though this may sometimes happen. What matters is that the 'representatives' are in a position to articulate the concerns and needs of their community and to ensure that this is kept informed of the work of the inter faith body. A structured body of this kind is increasingly needed in multi faith areas, even if complemented by additional more informal approaches.

Leeds Faiths Forum (LFF) began in 1998.* It is a representative body, the emphases of which complement those of Leeds' longer established inter faith body, **Leeds Concord Interfaith Fellowship** (which in general has more of a focus on spiritual dialogue), with which it works in partnership on various projects. Concord is open to individuals and groups to join but the Forum only has group membership. Much of the work is shared and there is a big overlap in the people involved in both groups. Concord attend all LFF Council meetings.

LFF links and shares information between the faith communities of Leeds. It serves as a forum for faith communities to enter into dialogue with each other and with relevant organs of government, including the City Council, Yorkshire Forward and the Regional Chamber for Yorkshire and Humberside. It has a strong focus on issues such as regeneration and faith based social action and it presently has Council members serving on the Board of the Local Strategic Partnership and on key strategy groups.

Continued overleaf

LFF is steered by a Council which includes Baha'is, Buddhists (from the Leeds Buddhist Council), Christians (Anglican, Catholic, Free Church, and the Black-led Churches), Hindus (from the main temple), Jews (from the Leeds Jewish Representative Council), Muslims (through the Leeds Muslim Forum), and Sikhs (through the Council of Sikh Gurdwaras (Leeds)). A City Council representative also attends LFF Council meetings.

* Formerly named Leeds Faith Communities Liaison Forum

The whole issue of 'representation' in the context of local inter faith activity is a difficult one. It is important not to expect perfection. The test is rather whether the pattern of representation which is achieved is good enough for its purpose and whether to have a representative body, albeit a less than perfect one, is better than not to have one at all.

Faith community involvement in local inter faith bodies

Information given by local groups to help with an enquiry to the Network office about the ways that local inter faith bodies involve the Jewish community gives an interesting picture of different options for involving faith communities generally:

- Direct membership of the local inter faith body by the local Jewish Representative Council (which links Jewish places of worship and other organisations in the area in question)

- Direct membership by the Jewish Representative Council, with JRC nominees on the local inter faith body's council

- Participation in the local inter faith body's Executive Committee by a representative from the Jewish Representative Council but no formal membership of the JRC as such

- Direct membership of the local inter faith body by one or more local synagogues from different sections of the community (Orthodox and Progressive)

- Individual Jewish members of the community as members of the inter faith body, without synagogues being in direct membership

- Regular contact by the inter faith body with local synagogues and their inclusion on its mailing list, but no formal membership arrangement

To some extent, the options reflect whether a local inter faith body has an arrangement for 'organisational' or 'group' membership. As a rule, local inter faith bodies set up with a representative role do have this, based on clear channels of nomination from the relevant faith community, whether from umbrella bodies or individual places of worship.

c) What area should our inter faith initiative cover?

It is not always obvious exactly what area a new initiative should cover. A small number, such as Suffolk Inter-Faith Resource and Lancashire Forum of Faiths, serve a large area such as a county or an area embracing several local authorities. At the opposite end of the spectrum, there are inter faith structures which serve one neighbourhood or area of a town or city. Most initiatives, however, cover one town, city or local authority area.

Within large conurbations, it is not uncommon to find a variety of geographically overlapping initiatives.

In Greater Manchester there is a **Manchester Interfaith Forum** which covers a number of local authority areas. There are also initiatives linked to particular local authority areas. For example, **Stockport Inter-Faith Network** was formed in 2003 to promote good relationships between people of different faiths, to foster community cohesion, and to act as a consultative forum within the Borough of Stockport. Within Greater Manchester's local authorities there are also some initiatives with a focus on a particular area, such as the longstanding inter faith body in the Whalley Range area of the City of Manchester.

Continued overleaf

South London has separate inter faith bodies serving Bexley, Croydon, Greenwich, Kingston upon Thames, Lambeth, Lewisham, Merton, Southwark, Stockwell, Wandsworth and Wimbledon. There is also a **South London Inter Faith Group** which is based on individual membership and has, since 1981, developed a network that spans a broad swathe of London south of the Thames. From the outset, it has had important relationships with more localised groups within its broad area, including organisations with a more representative basis. A useful feature has evolved around an annual inter faith walk, with visits to five or six faith communities on a summer Saturday, which is planned in conjunction with a different, more local, inter faith group each year.

Merseyside Council of Faiths works across Merseyside to articulate the concerns of religious communities and to provide channels of consultation with other groups and agencies and local government. Its programme also now incorporates the work of promoting inter faith understanding between individuals developed since the mid 80s by the Merseyside Inter Faith Group. In 2003, Liverpool Community Spirit was commissioned by Merseyside Council of Faiths and Liverpool Council for Voluntary Service to facilitate a faith community network specifically for Liverpool. **Liverpool Faith Network** is independent, Liverpool specific and has a strong focus on regeneration issues. It nominates two representatives for the Local Strategic Partnership.

It is desirable, if possible, to define the scope of any area-based initiative in such a way that it can involve residents, people who work in an area and people who regularly come to worship there. For this reason, bodies sometimes choose to make their membership open to religious groups or individuals active within an area.

The aims of **Forum of Faiths for Derby** include: "To affirm and develop good relations, inter-religious dialogue and mutual understanding between the various religious groups, organisations, initiatives and places of worship active in the city of Derby... To... maintain two-way communication and broad accountability with affiliates that constitute the 'Forum' and their constituencies, and to develop channels of information and communication with all religious groups, initiatives, organisations and places of worship active in city of Derby."

d) Who do we need to consult first?

Careful consultation with potential key people in the early stages is vital. If it is hoped to launch an initiative with long term prospects, their involvement from the outset is crucial so that they can help make it work or – if they are too busy for that – at least give it their blessing. It is far better to take longer at the planning stage than to move too fast and risk launching the council or group without careful advance preparation.

Chances of success are increased where letters are sent in advance to the individuals and organisations thought to be potentially most significant but are then followed up with phone calls and personal visits to discuss the possible initiative. Consider whether contact should be made by you or whether there is another person who might have particular impact because they are of the relevant faith. If there is such another person, their active involvement might give confidence to members of that faith who might not be sure whether this is an initiative to which it is worth giving their time.

It is impossible to overestimate the value of personal visits and phone conversations. This is especially important to keep local faith community leaders involved. Equally important is reassurance that the planned body will be one which will respect the integrity and distinctiveness of different faiths.

e) *How shall we make the initial links?*

You may be wanting to develop a relatively informal inter faith group based on individuals with a shared interest in inter faith matters. If so, you may already have friends and acquaintances of different faiths who could help set up such a group. If there is not already a nucleus of interested people you might ask at your own place of worship whether others have acquaintances they think might be interested in meeting for inter faith discussion. You could also contact local places of worship of the different faiths to see if any of their members are interested in the idea of an inter faith group or ask your local paper to run a short article about your interest in setting up a group and inviting others to a first meeting. Local radio might also run an item.

f) *Which local faith organisations need to be on board at the outset to ensure that the initiative is well backed and high profile?*

If the plan is to develop a council or forum of faiths where representativeness matters, it is best to begin by consulting key figures from all the main faith communities. It is desirable to involve these people and ensure their commitment before widening the circle of participants. A letter, followed up by a phone call and a personal visit, usually works best. Different faith communities have different structures and religious personnel. It may be preferable in some cases to contact religious personnel where these are available (such as vicars, rabbis and imams), but it is also important in the case of many communities to involve the president or the chair of the management committee for the place of worship.

Be aware of the different groups and denominations within some traditions: it is not always the case that a faith can be appropriately represented by just one person. Where there are umbrella bodies, such as 'Churches Together' groupings, contact these at an early stage.

If you are uncertain what organisations or places of worship to contact at the outset, check on the internet or with your local authority or library whether there is a directory of local places of worship or you could look at the details of places of worship listed in *Religions in the UK: A Directory* (see under Resources: Publications).

It is also helpful at the outset to let the local authority, the Mayor, and any local Racial Equality Council know that an initiative of this kind is being planned. The Mayor might be willing to join faith community leaders in launching it when the time comes. Civic backing is important for any representative council of this kind. It gives public recognition and establishes the inter faith council as a point of contact and advice on matters of public policy and public services in the locality.

g) Who will make the project their top priority?

Initiatives generally need at least one person of good standing in their own faith community with sensitivity and organising skills for whom the initiative is a personal top priority. This is essential at the start up stage because someone has to keep an eye on the programme of personal visits, phone calls and follow up as the planning begins. This also remains important as the initiative develops.

This person may or may not be the person who chairs any initial meetings to discuss a possible new group or council. It is advisable to invite a religious leader with good local standing to chair any initial discussions. This helps ensure the process is taken seriously.

Where a local authority is involved in an initiative of this kind, it may be the case that a member of its staff can assist in the establishment and servicing of this. This has happened in a number of areas (see the case study overleaf).

Forum of Faiths Kensington and Chelsea has been running since early 2002. It developed out of the Chief Executive of the Royal Borough of Kensington and Chelsea's meetings with Borough Deans. It has participation from eight faith traditions and has an elected chair and two vice-chairs. All its meetings are open ones. The Forum has become an independent, multi faith body which is used as a sounding board by many different Council departments (and by others such as the police) who are given slots to come and speak with the Forum at its meetings. It also carries out project work, such as working to establish a women's dialogue group and looking at chaplaincy issues and work with young people. Royal Borough of Kensington and Chelsea's Community Relations Section volunteered the time and support of its Community Information and Initiatives Officer who has, since the outset, had responsibility for servicing the Forum.

1   Breakdowns of faith community membership by local authority area for England and Wales can be found at www.statistics.gov.uk/census2001

5 | Developing effective local inter faith initiatives

Effective local inter faith initiatives are ones which serve well the needs of their particular areas. They may be of many kinds. Whether your organisation is just starting out or is an existing body reviewing its pattern of work and membership, the following checklist may be helpful. Some questions are particularly relevant for organisations which are planning to have a 'representative' role and a formal structure but are less likely to apply to an informal group. It is important to be clear at the outset which of these it is hoped to establish.

Aims and names
- What are our main aims?
- What shall we call ourselves?

Times and places
- Where shall we meet?
- When shall we meet ?

Developing a successful programme
- Are there any 'ground rules' that it is helpful to use?
- What sorts of events and activities do we want to run?
- What sort of role, if any, do we want to play in relation to external bodies such as the local authority?

Membership and structures
- Do we need a committee?
- Do we need 'officers' such as chair, vice-chair, secretary, treasurer?
- If we are setting up a more formal 'forum' or 'council', how will faith body members be nominated by their communities?
- Which faith communities will be involved?

Continued overleaf

Membership and structures continued

- Do we want to have honorary office bearers (eg presidents or patrons) drawn from senior faith leaders who want to give their support and endorsement even if they cannot attend regularly?
- Should we have both individual and group membership?
- Do we want a constitution?

Money matters

- Where will financial support come from?
- Will 'in kind' support be available (such as local authority staff time or venues)?

Volunteers, employees and premises

- How will our local inter faith organisation be serviced?
- Do we need an office or centre?

Making our work known

- Should we produce a newsletter and have a website?
- How do we put our work across to local people through the media?

Keeping a good thing going

- How will we ensure that our new local inter faith body is sustained and developed and responds well to changing circumstances over the years?

6 | Aims and Names

What are our aims?

Local inter faith bodies vary to some degree in their aims. The survey carried out by the Network in 2003 found a wide range of aims among respondents.[1] Here are a sample of aims from existing bodies which may be helpful at the early stages of developing a new initiative or when reviewing the work of an existing initative. In some cases these overlap but because precise wording can be important different examples are given. When a new initiative is being launched, discussing and clarifying its aims is a good way of helping to encourage a sense of shared ownership.

Some local inter faith body aims

- to promote and maintain harmonious relations between people of different faiths in the town

- to promote knowledge, understanding and mutual respect between the followers of different religions within our city

- to break down barriers of prejudice

- to work together to overcome ignorance, fear and misunderstanding between faiths

- to promote understanding and friendship between persons of different faiths

- to heal painful memories of religious bigotry and intolerance and attempt to create new memories born of new experiences of peace, harmony and understanding

- to explore shared values

- to be an inspiration and resource for the local community

- to work together for harmony and cohesion in the community

- to bring faith groups together for dialogue

Continued overleaf

- to make a public 'statement' by demonstrating that people of different faiths can talk and listen to one another

- to involve faith and cultural groups in the civic life of the borough

- to develop projects, programmes and events that improve inter faith education and outreach within the borough

- to arrange occasions at which we experience each other's worship, witness each other's ceremonies, enter into dialogue with one another and celebrate our common commitment to spiritual values

- to enable the Council and local faith groups to discuss matters of mutual concern/interest

- to provide a means for faith communities to speak and act together on social and community issues

- to improve the quality of life for local people by working together on agreed projects demonstrating partnership between different faiths

- to be a representative voice for the faith communities

- to encourage dialogue and provide an opportunity for faith based organisations to network with each other and the Council

What's in a name?

People often like to find a name for a new initiative very early on. There can be much debate about names!

Names of initiatives differ, although they usually include the name of the town or area. Common names for the more informal groups are 'inter faith group' or 'fellowship of faiths' or 'sharing of faiths group'. The terms 'council of faiths' or 'forum of faiths' usually indicate that a local inter faith body takes particularly seriously the importance of active representative involvement of the main faith communities in the area. However, the name of an organisation does not always reflect in this way its precise role. There are 'groups' which operate more like 'councils' and *vice versa*.

'Multi faith' is an expression normally used to make a descriptive statement about a project or organisation to indicate that many faiths are involved. Occasionally, bodies opt to use names such as 'multi faith forum' or 'forum of faiths' because they want to emphasise the aspect of faiths working side by side on social issues more strongly than their interaction. The Network's survey of local inter faith activity came across this phenomenon in areas where new bodies with a link to a local authority or Local Strategic Partnership were keen to send a message that their agenda was not 'theological' or 'dialogical' as they thought this might be off putting.[2]

Just a few of the names chosen by local inter faith bodies:

Council of Faiths, Inter Faith Council, Forum of Faiths, Inter Faith Forum, Inter Faith Association, Inter Faith Group, Interfaith Society, Interfaith Fellowship, Sharing of Faiths, Friends of Faith, Multi Faith Forum, Multi Faith Partnership, Inter Faith Action, Round Table of Religions.

It is important to note, however, that even where the 'inter faith' terminology is avoided, faith and multi faith forums still usually have a signicant inter faith dimension to their work in that they include the aim of developing understanding between different groups as part of community cohesion. Good examples of this are Glasgow Forum of Faiths and the North Lincolnshire Multi Faith Partnership (see overleaf).

In a number of areas 'faith networks' have emerged to assist with enabling dialogue between faith groups and Local Strategic Partnerships or Community Empowerment Networks. As the name suggests, the focus of such bodies often tends to be on information sharing and contacts.

Glasgow Forum of Faiths brings together civic authorities and leaders of various faith communities:

- to work for the good of Glasgow

- to promote mutual understanding of the teachings, traditions and practices of the different faith communities in the Glasgow area, including an awareness of their common ground and a respect for their distinctive features

- to recognise the problems experienced in the practice of any faith within the local community and to work together for their solution

- to work for harmony and peaceful coexistence and to promote dialogue and friendship between people of different faiths

- to oppose prejudice wherever it exists in the local community

- to work with faith groups and other inter faith organisations for shared religious values within civic society

---

The North Lincolnshire Multi Faith Partnership has been operating in its present multi faith form since 2001. It is used by North Lincolnshire Council as a consultative body and is also often used as a consultative body by external partners such as the police and organisations from the voluntary sector. The Multi Faith Partnership's aims are:

- to provide a forum exploring faith issues and developing dialogue between faith communities

- to help develop mutual respect amongst people of all different faiths in the North Lincolnshire area

- to help raise awareness of faiths and faith issues amongst the community of North Lincolnshire

- to aid understanding and tolerance for both young and old people in the faith communities

Inter faith, inter-faith, or interfaith?

Some groups and councils use 'interfaith' in their name. Others prefer to use 'inter faith' or 'inter-faith' because they are concerned that the use of the single word 'interfaith' could give the impression that the different faiths are being mixed up or their distinctness played down. It is important to be sensitive to the impact words can have because they can affect whether people of various faiths feel comfortable with plans for an inter faith initiative.

1 *Local Inter Faith Activity in the UK: A Survey*, Inter Faith Network, 2003, pp 22-24.

2 *Local Inter Faith Activity in the UK*, p 24 and p 91.

7 | Times and places

It is essential that people should feel comfortable about participating in a group's activities. Choice of venue and timing of meetings have a major bearing on this – especially for newcomers to inter faith encounter.

Where is a good place to meet?

It is important to find venues which make participants feel at ease. Some have found that in the early days of a new initiative, when members as yet are without a strong sense of each other's views and sensitivities, it can be helpful to meet on neutral ground at venues such as community centres or town halls. However, a number of local inter faith bodies meet at faith community venues but rotate the venue to avoid undue identification with one particular faith tradition and to ensure that a wider sense of ownership and involvement can develop.

> Our forum meetings are held at different faith centres with part of the evening being given over to getting to know not just the particular faith, but the particular community. The rest of the evening is given over to discussing a main theme, such as health or youth. The format has engendered an understanding of the local community and a sharing of common concerns that face religious congregations. This has enabled us to work together to address some of these concerns. *Dudley Borough Interfaith Network*

When using faith community venues, be aware of some possible sensitivities. Places of worship can be pleasant and appropriate meeting places, but it is important to discover just where the 'sacred' or explicitly religious area of a faith community's building may be and which parts are considered, by contrast, as appropriate for ordinary meetings. In some traditions it may be obvious what these areas are, by the fact that removal of shoes or covering of the head may be requested before entry. In modern and adapted church buildings, the situation may be less clear because meetings without a specifically religious purpose sometimes take place even in the church itself, as distinct from its church hall – although most such churches still do retain a particular sacred area.

Participants should also be made aware of the do's and don't's of a particular place of worship – such as not carrying any tobacco products on your person in a gurdwara – which apply to conduct in the building as a whole.

See www.interfaith.org.uk or www.multifaithnet.org for guidelines on visiting places of worship of particular faiths.

Where there is a distinction between the kinds of spaces within a building, the least 'sacred' or worship-focused area is best for inter faith meetings. Participants of different religions are likely to feel more comfortable about meeting in these 'day to day' areas. An example might be the community centre attached to a Hindu mandir. Some participants may not, on the other hand, feel completely comfortable about a visit which would involve them in entering a sacred space where they might feel obliged to offer respect to another's sacred symbols (or might be worried about causing offence in refusing to do so for religious reasons). Genuine reservations are not uncommon, although sometimes there is a reluctance to express them openly in case offence is caused. It is important to be clear about people's views and to ensure that participants do not feel in some way compromised or left open to criticism from others within their faith community. It is also important to note that some religious groups will expect people to dress modestly or for women not to enter certain areas at particular times.

> Q: A member of our council mentioned recently that he had felt rather put on the spot by being offered specially blessed food at a place of worship not belonging to his own tradition because he was unsure of the religious significance.
>
> A: It is not just words that can make people feel uncomfortable. Being unexpectedly asked, for example, to participate in a clearly religious activity or being offered food that has been blessed in the context of a ritual of a faith to which the recipient does not belong can cause anxiety. It is important that expectations of both hosts and guests are made very clear in advance and that no one feels obliged to participate in ways which make them feel uncomfortable. The significance of any food to be offered needs to be made clear.

Check the calendar

Check that events being planned do not clash with one of the key festivals and fasts of a group that you are hoping to involve. Preparation for festivals sometimes begins some days ahead of the date listed in the calendar, and this can affect people's ability to attend events. The annual *Shap Calendar of Religious Festivals* (see under Resources: Publications) is a vital planning tool and comes with a booklet explaining the significance of each festival. The dates of the festivals of all faiths are based on their own calendars. These are, in many cases, linked to the solar and lunar cycles and change each year in relation to the Gregorian calendar used in the UK, so it is very important to check these each year. There are also multi faith calendars on the internet, such as the BBC calendar at www.bbc.co.uk/religion/interactive/calendar/index.shtml

Members should be asked to indicate which of the calendar dates are best avoided when scheduling meetings. Two faith traditions have extended fasting periods which it is a courtesy to bear in mind. Consult with Muslim members about the timing of any events during the period of Ramadan when practising Muslims fast from before dawn until sunset and when early evening events can be difficult for them to attend because of the time of prayer and breaking of the fast. Similarly, Baha'is fast from sunrise to sunset during the period 2-20 March, the Baha'i Fast, and this should be taken into account in scheduling meetings. Some Christians fast during the period of Lent, and in particular on Ash Wednesday. Members of other faiths, such as Hindus and Jews, also fast at particular times.

The inter faith group or council may want to mark or attend the different festivals of the faiths. If so, it is important to consult well in advance with the faith community to check how this might fit into the pattern of their community's festivities.

Being aware of members' patterns of religious observance

Inter faith groups and councils succeed best where they take account of the religious observances of their various members. From late afternoon on Friday until sunset on Saturday is problematic for observant Jews in relation to events involving travel and what could be construed as 'work' (though interpretations of this vary within different parts of the community). Fridays can also be difficult for observant Muslims, and especially for imams, because of the importance of the Friday midday prayer. For churchgoing Christians, Sunday mornings can be difficult (some Christians, such as Seventh Day Adventists, keep Saturday as their Sabbath). Other faith communities will also have days which are significant for them, although these may vary. Members of all faith traditions linked by your group or council should be carefully consulted about the days that are significant for them.

During day-long events, it is helpful to leave times when those who wish can retire separately for prayer or meditation, and to ensure that there is a place for this. Muslims are required to pray five times a day at specific times and men and women pray separately. There is some flexibility of time according to circumstances, but it is necessary to provide space for prayer at the correct times, as well as suitable washing facilities. It is also desirable to offer a sheet for covering the floor for prayer.

Because of the practical difficulty for many people of not being able to take time off during the working week, weekend events may prove necessary. If you are planning a weekend event, it is important to check with members how they personally feel about attending on these days or about their participation during particular parts of the timetable.

> "Sometimes I wish there was an eighth day in the week for inter faith events!"
> *Comment from a local inter faith organiser*

8 | Developing a successful programme

A successful programme is one which includes an appropriate and interesting range of activities, which is conducted in a way which reflects the commitment of a local inter faith organisation to developing mutual respect and understanding, and which participants from all the different faiths enjoy.

Ethos

It is particularly important to establish a context where people feel that their faith identity is respected and where listening is as important as putting one's own views across. Very clear ground rules should always be established from the earliest days of a group or council about what are, and are not, acceptable ways to share one's beliefs. The Inter Faith Network's code, *Building Good Relations with People of Different Faiths and Beliefs*, which is printed at Annex B at the end of this guide, gives some helpful guidelines for encounter. The group or council may wish formally to adopt this code as a shared understanding of the issues.

Q: We are worried that one of our members is abusing the dialogue situation and is using our meetings to seek converts.

A: We are all mutually influenced by our encounters in life and we sometimes seek to persuade each other about our views in the context of our day to day interactions. But in inter faith meetings we need to be very careful that there are no deliberate attempts to undermine the religious identity of a partner in dialogue. In inter faith dialogue, each person can rightly expect that differences of faith identity will be respected. Sometimes a presenter at a meeting may not realise they are crossing what some of their audience experience as a line between explanation and seeking to convert. When this happens, members must feel able to indicate gently but firmly that they are finding the situation problematic.

Activities

No two local inter faith organisations are exactly alike in their work and they carry out a very wide range of activities. This is the list of activities reported in *Local Inter Faith Activity in the UK: A Survey* (p 26) with an indication of what percentage of bodies were carrying out the different types:

Activity	%
Multi faith dialogue	82
Promoting harmonious community relations	79
Discussion meetings on religious topics	78
Discussion meetings on social topics	66
Inter faith awareness raising	63
Assisting in multi faith civic ceremonies	60
Social gatherings	60
Prayer/worship	57
Shared meals	53
Acting as a consultative forum on local issues for local government	52
Educational events/exhibitions	50
Peace walks/multi faith pilgrimages	48
Providing advice/assistance to public bodies	48
Making statements on current issues	45
Sending representatives to serve on local strategic initiatives	44
Sending speakers to schools	34
Involvement in regeneration/neighbourhood renewal	33
Events for young people	24
Bilateral dialogue	23
Diversity training	18
Trilateral dialogue	16
Women's meetings	12
Environmental projects	7

This section of the guide looks at some of these areas of work and gives a number of examples drawn from local inter faith bodies around the UK. Further examples will be found in *Local Inter Faith Activity in the UK: A Survey* (see under Resources: Publications) and on the Network's website: www.interfaith.org.uk

A well structured, varied and lively programme will maintain the interest of members and encourage the involvement of new people.

Discussion meetings on social and religious topics

The backbone of most local inter faith bodies' programmes is discussion meetings on social and religious topics.

Representative councils of faiths are likely to have agendas which focus primarily on current issues of concern to the different local faith communities. Such an agenda might include, for example, the provision of appropriate pastoral care and food in local hospitals, facilities for local burials which meet the requirements of different faiths and the approach of the local educational authority to issues relating to the faith identity of pupils.

The work of local councils of faiths is also likely to include business meetings with representatives of local government, the local health authority and similar public authorities.

Most councils of faiths also arrange meetings with more general themes. In cases where other meetings of the council are normally restricted to nominated faith community leaders, these more general meetings are likely to be open to wider participation. Also, more informal local inter faith groups often address more 'social' issues in addition to specifically religious topics. There will therefore often be an overlap in the kinds of themes and issues discussed by different kinds of local inter faith organisations.

Often, themes cut across religious, social, and cultural boundaries. For example, a common theme is the relationship between the older and younger generations and the transmission of religious tradition and belief.

Whatever the topic, it is important to ensure that members of all the faiths represented in the group have a chance to offer their reflections and, during the year's programme, to be the main presenter.

Some frequently chosen topics for meetings are understandings of different faiths of:

- God or the nature of Ultimate Reality
- Prayer and meditation
- Worship
- Fasting
- Festivals
- Attitudes to other faiths
- The life cycle
- The virtuous life
- Saints or holy men and women
- Scriptures
- Religion, peace and violence
- Music
- The roles of men and women
- The environment
- Values
- Human rights
- Money and business ethics
- Disadvantages or discrimination experienced by different faith groups
- Economic and social needs of the area
- Religious education and collective worship in local schools
- Provision for people of different faiths in hospitals, prisons and other public institutions

Some groups have a programme pattern where a particular topic is chosen for a series and each faith provides a speaker for one meeting in the series. 15-20 minutes' presentation followed by an hour or so's discussion is generally a successful format. Another approach is to use a panel discussion at a single meeting.

We held an event called 'Endings?' to discuss beliefs and practices related to death. It was a follow-up to an earlier meeting on 'Beginning, Belonging and Continuing'. Participants split up into groups of 5 or 6 to discuss their beliefs about what happens to beings at death and after; what this means for our obligations to those dying and those who have died; and our attitudes to our own mortality. At the end they reassembled in one group, and shared thoughts that had come out of the discussions. Particularly timely, in the wake of the Tsunami tragedy, was the question of how communities cope with widespread loss of life, caused by atrocity or natural disaster. *Manchester Interfaith Forum*

Some topic areas can be difficult. In particular, if it is decided to focus on a particular religious or political conflict in another country there needs to be very careful consideration of how to ensure a balance of perspectives and to secure a discussion which does not cause offence or hurt to some of the participants.

It is helpful to avoid mixing topical discussion or social programmes with 'management' matters. It may seem, on the face of it, a good use of time to combine meeting functions but it can actually be off-putting and detract from the event.

Visiting places of worship

Groups frequently arrange visits to particular local places of worship to learn more about the faith in question. Sometimes they have ongoing visit programmes (see the case study overleaf).

> Our continuing programme of visits to churches, mosques, temples, gurdwaras, synagogues, centres, and educational and hospital chaplaincies, together with the attendant talks about the faiths, has as a whole served to inform the group's members, and the members of the institutions being visited, and helped us to deepen our mutual understanding and form friendships.
> *Lancashire Forum of Faiths*

Multi faith walks and pilgrimages

Some local inter faith bodies arrange annual multi faith pilgrimages or walks. These serve a number of different functions in that they enable people to see the local places of worship and meet people of other faiths and they are a very visible symbol of inter faith cooperation and friendship. Well known examples include the Bradford Peace Walk, the Edinburgh Inter-Faith Association inter faith pilgrimage and the Wolverhampton 'bus pilgrimage' (which allows everyone to take part even if they cannot walk far).

> **Coventry peace walk** The 2004 walk was arranged by **Coventry Multi-Faith Forum** and started at the Multi-Faith Centre, in Priory Row. It began with members of a number of major faith groups getting together and saying prayers and reading from holy books. The walk around the city centre went to Coventry Cathedral, Eagle Street Mosque, the Shree Krishna Temple and Gurdwara Gurunanak Parkash Gurdwara. The BBC reporter accompanying the walkers said: "At each place we learnt a little about each religion and heard the repeated message that all seek understanding and unity.... The walk was a very enjoyable and unusual way to start the weekend. It was at turns solemn and inspiring but always fascinating and thoughtful. The group was as varied as the places we visited and was a genuine mix of races and religions, all generously giving their time to make the most of the event. It was a great way to start Coventry Peace Month and to mark the city's important role as a centre for unity."

Westminster Interfaith pilgrimage One of the best known inter faith pilgrimages in the UK is organised by a Roman Catholic initiative in the Diocese of Westminster: **Westminster Interfaith**. For twenty years it has arranged an annual Pilgrimage for Peace to bring together people of different religious traditions. Members of local inter faith groups in the area also take part in the pilgrimage. Their Director says:

"The Pilgrimage for Peace is a walk through the streets of London which follows a different route each year, taking in various boroughs of the city. Buddhist monks and nuns of the Nipponzan Myohoji Order usually lead the way beating their peace drums. The route is marked by 'stations' or stops at the places of worship of different religions. Buddhist viharas, Christian churches, Hindu mandirs, Jewish synagogues, Muslim mosques, Sikh gurdwaras all welcome the pilgrims. On a recent occasion a Jain 'house mandir' also welcomed them. Prayers are offered, refreshments served, and strength restored for the continuing march.

The Westminster Interfaith peace pilgrimage serves a double purpose. For those who participate, it provides an opportunity for new discoveries. The host communities are able to receive their guests according to their own traditions, and to present themselves on their own terms. In an even more personal manner, those who are walking side by side are led to share their stories like Chaucer's pilgrims on their way to Canterbury.

The pilgrims, with their varied dress reflecting their different religious traditions, also serve as a symbol to onlookers, saying to the community at large, so often beset by racial and religious tensions, that it is possible for people of different beliefs to act in harmony. Where there is respect and understanding, peace is possible."

'Faith trails'

Recently, some local inter faith bodies such as Bolton Interfaith Council and Merseyside Council of Faiths have been involved in helping develop 'faith trails' or 'faith walks' for their areas which enable the general public to visit and come to know about different local places of worship.[1]

Multi faith civic ceremonies

In multi faith areas it is increasingly common for civic religious events to reflect this religious diversity and for local inter faith bodies to be invited to advise on events and to provide participants. Sometimes they play an even more extensive role where there are regular civic events designed especially to highlight inter faith cooperation and community.

There is an annual 'civic celebration of community' attended by the Mayor and many faith groups. From about 1974-95 there was an annual United Nations act of dedication for peace. **Cambridge Inter-Faith Group** (CIFG) came into existence following a discussion at the 1980 meeting and were active participants. From 2001 onwards the 'celebration' has been the initiative of CIFG and they organise it by writing to various faith communities and the Mayor asking them to contribute. Around a dozen faith groups now contribute.

There has been an annual civic inter faith celebration in Bristol since 1993. It is run jointly by the Lord Mayor's Office and **Bristol Inter Faith Group** (BIFG). Faith communities offer readings, music, drama and prayers on a theme suggested by BIFG. The event takes place at the Council House and includes a buffet meal. Hospitality, printing, and publicity costs are met by the Lord Mayor's Office.

Prayer or worship

Many local inter faith bodies experience prayer or meditation as an important part of their existence, but there are particular sensitivities about this. Most common is shared silent prayer. Also frequently found is the pattern of sequential offerings of prayers from members of different faiths. This is sometimes called 'serial prayer' because members of different religions serially pray or offer a reading relevant to the theme to which others listen, but in which they do not actively participate; rather, prayer is offered individually by members of the gathering in a way which respects the integrity of each tradition.

Why is it difficult having shared spoken prayers? When spoken joint prayers are used, there is always the danger that people find themselves voluntarily or involuntarily joining in what appears to be worship of a divinity who is not recognisably as they understand the Divine and feeling pressed to participate even though they would prefer not to do so. Also, non theists (such as Buddhists) can be put into an awkward situation by assumptions that all religions acknowledge a Divine Being. Likewise, for traditions where the Divine is understood wholly or partly in feminine or in impersonal terms, the constant use of masculine or personal terms may prove alienating. Given these possibilities for misunderstanding and offence, it is important to sound out carefully how individual members feel about shared spoken prayer, before it becomes part of a group's life.[2]

We organise an evening of prayer and food annually and invite representatives from our different faith communities to lead a section of prayer. We also include the possibility for other people to contribute a reading or a prayer. Last October we made a special effort to involve the Mosque Committee in the planning, along with our Sharing of Faiths Committee ... and the publicity went out in our joint name. This was a first and very encouraging. *Wycombe Sharing of Faiths*

Social gatherings and shared meals

Family events and gatherings are important to engage all ages. Meals are often part of this (see Annex A 'Catering for multi faith events').

Altrincham Interfaith Group (AIG) held an inter faith meal in the Stamford Hall, at the Altrincham Grammar School for Boys. Each community brought along food to share with others, which was served in a buffet style, allowing people to try one another's food. Families from each of the faiths were seated together in a pre-arranged seating plan to encourage people to get to know one another and improve understanding of one another's traditions. Each faith group also said their own prayers for starting the meal. After the meal, representatives from each group gave a five-minute talk each on the meaning of social responsibility from their faith perspective. AIG went on to hold a family weekend which included a picnic in the grounds of Tatton Hall in Cheshire. On one of the hottest days of the year, over 120 people from babies to grandparents turned up for what everyone agreed was a fantastic day.

Working with schools

Some local inter faith bodies help with arranging visits of school pupils to places of worship or arranging special educational events.

Large numbers of students and pupils and their teachers have participated in the visits to places of worship organised by the **Wolverhampton Inter Faith Group** in partnership with local faith communities. The visitors not only gain first-hand experience of another faith, albeit very briefly, but also receive explanations from someone from that particular community. In order to make their experience meaningful, we have produced *Faith Lives*, resource material for schools and other agencies. This education pack tries to encapsulate the essential beliefs and practices of different faiths in the local context.

> We organised 'Spring for Peace' – an art, poetry and essay
> competition for mainstream and weekend religion schools. The
> 300+ entries were displayed at a Saturday exhibition, alongside
> general exhibits from all the faiths. An afternoon presentation by
> young people, again a mixture of mainstream and religion schools,
> looked at the theme of peace from various religious perspectives.
> All of our members' faiths were involved and the event drew a
> fair number of people, boosted by shoppers drawn in by the
> young people giving out leaflets and playing trumpets in the
> neighbouring shopping centre. *Harrow Inter Faith Council*

Inter faith issues are now very much part of RE in many schools.
For some local inter faith bodies, an important part of their
outreach is sending speakers from different faiths to talk to pupils
in local schools. A few, such as the Building Bridges Project in
Pendle, have staff specifically employed to carry out this area of
work or, like Suffolk Inter-Faith Resource, employ tutors of
different faiths to work with schools. Most rely on volunteers of
different faiths.

> **Tower Hamlets Inter Faith Forum** has been working in
> partnership with secondary schools and the SACRE to develop a
> model to support religious education and community cohesion by
> encouraging faith leaders to visit schools. Three schools are
> piloting the project. A workshop took place led by the Head of RE
> at Mulberry School to look at how visits would be structured and
> to encourage faith leaders to be volunteers for the pilot. The idea
> is that volunteers will visit the classroom in pairs, as part of a
> lesson planned by the class teacher. They will be able to give faith
> perspectives and will also be role models showing respect and
> understanding across religions.

In England and Wales, the local Standing Advisory Council for
Religious Education (SACRE) helps shape the Local Agreed
Syllabus which determines the pattern of RE in local schools.

It also carries out some other activities to assist with the development of RE in schools and these are likely to include liaison with local faith communities. Recently the National Association of SACREs (NASACRE) has initiated a programme to encourage local SACREs to be involved in holding young inter faith forums.

It is helpful to be in touch with your local SACRE and some local inter faith bodies actually build such cooperation into their aims. For example, one of Brent Interfaith's aims is: "To liaise with the local SACRE and promote understanding and common values of world religions and religious communities in schools."

Events for young people

Local inter faith organisations are increasingly seeking ways to involve young people in inter faith activities. A widely used resource for young people is the Network's inter faith youth action guide *Connect: Different Faiths Shared Values* (see under Resources: Publications). Among the ideas suggested in the guide are a number which point young people to local inter faith groups as knowledgeable resources.

In 2005, **Birmingham Council of Faiths** held a youth event, 'Living Between Cultures', in partnership with **Birmingham Youth Service**. This was described as a 'youth forum' and brought together young people of various faiths – recruited by both BCF and BYS – for an evening of discussion in Birmingham City Council House. Young participants talked about some of the pressures they experienced in living in a secular culture and following a religious tradition. As a result of the event, there are plans to try and set up a youth inter faith group run by BYS with an annual contact with BCF.

If your local inter faith body plans to work directly with young people under the age of 18 it needs to develop a Child Protection Policy. Advice on this is to be found in two Home Office documents *Safe from Harm: A Code of Practice for Safeguarding the Welfare of Children in Voluntary Organisations in England*

and Wales and *Caring for Young People and the Vulnerable* (see under Resources: Publications). Very helpful is the NSPCC's guidance, *StopCheck: A Step by Step Guide for Organisations to Safeguard Children* (see under Resources: Publications). Policies are not hard to develop, nor are vetting procedures too onerous, but some groups will prefer to work with older young people or to work with other agencies such as schools or youth organizations where their staff take primary responsibility for ensuring the well being of the children.

Some local inter faith organisations make links with local colleges and universities. Many have staff and students from a diversity of religious traditions who may not easily find out what is going on in their local area and would be glad to hear about inter faith activities (and possibly to participate if their institution does not have an inter faith group of its own). They can also be sources of speakers, although it is important that any speaker from an academic context – as from any context – is one who is acceptable to faith community members of the tradition to which the speaker's presentation relates.

Some institutions of Higher Education, such as Warwick University, now have their own inter faith groups or forums.

Exhibitions and inter faith awareness raising

Putting together an exhibition of local places of worship and faith communities can help create greater inter faith understanding.

Living Faith in Wolverhampton was created by the **Wolverhampton Inter-Faith Group** (WIFG) as a contribution to its basic purposes: to encourage and enable people of different faiths and cultures to understand and respect one another as 'people of faith' and to encourage the general understanding of the importance of faith and its communities for the general community. Support and sponsorship were provided by Dunns Imaging Group plc, the University of Wolverhampton's School of Art and Design, and the West Midlands Police Authority. It can be seen on-line at www.wlv.ac.uk/chaplaincy/photoex

Faiths in Nottingham is a touring exhibition about different religions in the city, forming a set with a more detailed *Faiths File* leaflet pack. It was launched in October 2003, and has been on display in schools, places of worship and at the Nottingham Prison. It has already been on display at various public events in 2005 and is scheduled to be used in one of the city's major companies later this year. The exhibition consists of one panel about each of nine faiths (Bahá'í, Brahma Kumaris, Buddhism, Christianity, Hinduism, Islam, Judaism, Quaker, Sikhism), one about Nottingham Inter Faith Council, and two about our recent projects, all mounted on a display stand. The leaflet pack contains a two-sided A4 sheet about each of the nine faiths, printed in two colours, in a full colour card folder. *Nottingham Inter Faith Council*

'Faith fairs' where different faith communities have display stalls to give information about their beliefs and practices are also popular. Sometimes there is a special theme, such as 'winter festivals' or 'festivals of light'.

Diversity training

Some local inter faith organisations such as Leicester Council of Faiths and Suffolk Inter-Faith Resource undertake diversity training. This is somewhat different from 'inter faith awareness raising' in that it has the goal of helping public and corporate bodies learn more about the beliefs and practices of people of different faiths. Sometimes this diversity work extends to helping employers respond to recent legislation and employment regulations which have a bearing on issues of discrimination in employment and in the provision of goods and services.

Special events

Special events are helpful every year or so to increase the profile of the group.

When planning events it is helpful to bear in mind that programmes can get over full. It is as well to avoid the kind of over ambitious planning which assumes that the small troupe of children acting out a scene from the life of their faith's founder will actually be on and off stage in ten minutes or that the panellist on 'my faith's view of care for the environment' will want to wind up at the five minute mark.

A good rule of thumb is to allow one third more time than you initially thought the programme needed! If it is particularly important that people arrive exactly on time, then explain why in the mailing about the event.

When planning special events, it is always important to discuss with all those involved whether there are particular sensitivities which need to be kept in mind. For example, musical contributions and dancing please many people but for others certain types of music and many forms of dance may be incompatible with their religious beliefs and practices.

To mark **Bedford Council of Faiths**' recent acquisition of charity status a gathering of 120 people attended a celebration at The Place, Bradgate Road. A variety of food generously given by the different communities was enjoyed by guests and music contributed by different faiths provided a tapestry of background sound. There were speeches by the High Sheriff of Bedfordshire and the Director of the Inter Faith Network who provided a perspective on the national inter faith scene. Members of ten different faiths gave presentations conveying their essential beliefs and values. The chair of Bedford Council of Faiths presided over the event, inviting organisations to link with BCoF, and to benefit from its experience and knowledge of local religious and cultural diversity.

Some special events organised by local inter faith bodies have a fund raising dimension.

> We realised that all our communities raise money for charitable work of various kinds. We decided that this was something we could share in the form of organising a special event. Through deciding what to do and how to do it we would also learn more about each other. The outcome is an 'autumn bazaar' where small items will be sold and there will be demonstrations of skills such as Chinese paper folding. We are linking with One World Week, which includes United Nations Day. The funds will go internationally to three different UNICEF children's projects.
> *Telford and Wrekin Interfaith Group*

Joint meetings with other organisations

Local inter faith bodies sometimes hold joint meetings and events in partnership with other organisations such as the Council of Christians and Jews, One World Week, Religions for Peace, Amnesty, the United Nations Association or a local environment group.

> We held a special event for One World Week event: "Peace Depends on Dialogue". After an introduction by the Group's co-ordinator, there was Indian classical dance, lighting of candles by invited individuals of the different faiths, a presentation from a Muslim specialist in inter faith relations, and a question period. The event also included songs and a special prayer for peace.
> *Wellingborough Multi Faith Group*
>
> ---
>
> We recently held a festival of faiths in collaboration with the Rotary Clubs of the Dundee area with presentations from most local faith communities. *Dundee Inter Faith Association*

Local inter faith bodies can play an important role in assisting on events such as Holocaust Memorial Day.

Members of all faiths and cultures came together to remember the victims of the Holocaust and of oppression and torture across the world at a ceremony on the steps of Blackburn Town Hall on King William Street in the town centre. This was arranged by **Blackburn with Darwen Interfaith Council**, whose chair led the ceremony, in partnership with the Borough Council. The Minister of Higher Crumsall and Higher Broughton Synagogue in Salford gave the main address. Following the Mayor's closing address, the faith representatives lit candles at a short ceremony as a sign of peace, unity and hope for the future.

Women's meetings

Members of a group or council may have differing attitudes to the roles and relationships of men and women. There can be variety even within one religious tradition according to how a group interprets that tradition and according to the cultural background in which their tradition has been practised. A Chasidic Jewish family will have a different dynamic from a Reform Jewish one. Anglicans may differ one from another concerning what they believe the Bible and tradition teach about the roles of Christian men and women. Within Islam, interpretations of the Qur'an and Shariah by the different legal schools mean that there is diversity of interpretation. However, modesty is an important concept in Islam for both women and men. Some interpret this to mean that single sex events should be the norm. Others interpret it to mean that meetings including both men and women in public contexts can take place provided that they are characterised by a careful, formal, and modest manner.

Within almost every religious tradition there are those who believe that women should not exercise a public leadership role, and there are those who believe they should. This can occasionally lead to awkwardness over finding women to speak or participate in multi faith events. Generally, the best rule is to proceed with courtesy and care in requesting speakers, and to try to accommodate requests for such arrangements as allowing a person's spouse or other family member to travel with them for reasons of propriety. There may be a case for holding occasional separate women's meetings under the aegis of the group as a way of providing a forum for those participants who could feel uncomfortable in a mixed gathering, for religious, cultural or personal reasons. Oldham Inter Faith Forum, for example, involves women as well as men in the main forum but has also helped form the Oldham Women's Inter Faith Network which meets separately and also gives input to the overall Forum.

In two cases, women's local inter faith initiatives have been established: Thames Gateway Women's Multifaith Forum and St Albans Interfaith Women's Group. There are also bilateral initiatives such as a women's Muslim-Christian dialogue group in Leicester and special issue focused groups like the multi faith Bradford Women for Peace.

A group of women from St Pius X Roman Catholic Church in the Royal Borough of Kensington and Chelsea (RBKC) recently visited the Muslim Cultural Heritage Centre and a meeting was arranged between them and some Muslim women who work at the Centre. The women found they had a lot in common to talk about and felt that anything that would help them to learn about each other's faiths would bring women of all faiths together to work for the common good of the whole community. Across the coming year, **Forum of Faiths Kensington and Chelsea** will be making arrangements to give women of all faiths linked to the Forum a chance to meet and talk together. The process will be serviced by the Community Relations Section of RBKC.

Working with the local authority, Local Strategic Partnership and other partnerships

For a number of local inter faith and multi faith bodies, an important dimension of their work is giving input on areas such as local authority policy and service delivery and working with the LSP and Community Network.[3]

> Because of our seat on the Local Strategic Partnership, the voice of faith has been heard in the handling of the theme 'Engaging with Communities' which is undertaken by the working group which services the LSP. It is also heard on various committees in the town such as the Environmental Sub Group of the LSP and the Land, Assets and Property Management Partnership which is an innovatory group led by the borough. Other 'political' engagements have grown out of this – including liaison at regional and sub-regional levels. *Northampton Faiths Forum*

Providing advice and assistance to public bodies

Local inter faith bodies can be invaluable resources for bodies such as hospitals and services such as the police or fire service. Some have worked closely with these to assist on projects to serve users of different faiths. In a few areas, such as the London Borough of Enfield, public bodies such as the police have not simply consulted with local inter faith groups, they have been key movers in developing local inter faith initiatives.

> Having been involved for some time in the community involvement side of Probationer Training, we have become close partners with Suffolk Constabulary and are helping to develop the inter-faith/multi-cultural dimension of police training at all levels. We serve on the Police Diversity Programme Board and are a first port of call for support and advice in emergencies and various matters connected to community safety and cohesion. We now receive some funding from the police to support our work with Muslims. *Suffolk Inter-Faith Resource*

In recent years, a number of inter faith groups and councils have been working with their local hospitals and hospices to ensure that these can meet the needs of patients of different faiths. This can involve: helping find a list of clergy and lay people of the various faiths to be involved in chaplaincy and visiting; advising on dietary issues; discussing matters such as requirements for single sex wards; and offering training on the faith aspects of diversity.

North Kirklees Inter Faith Council supported the development of the new faith centre at Dewsbury Hospital providing rooms for prayer and counselling for members of all faiths, with eg appropriate washing facilities.

Medway Inter Faith Action Forum (MIFAF) has been working with staff at the Demelza House Children's Hospice to develop links between the hospice and local religious communities. Its programme began with a training evening for care workers at the hospice. Representatives from some of the local faith communities gave talks to staff. These started by outlining the basic beliefs and structures of their religions before moving on to speak about the beliefs and practices surrounding death, dying and bereavement in their different traditions. Staff found the evening to be very helpful and moves are now being made to build on these early links that have been made between the hospice and local faith communities.

It is hoped that MIFAF will be able to offer further assistance to the hospice as it develops its 'quiet room' into an area with resources for a number of different faiths to use. In addition plans are being made for staff training days that will include visits to local places of worship. This contact will give the hospice a number of religious communities to draw upon in the event that patients and their families need faith support beyond that which is currently offered by the chaplain. It is hoped that this will be the start of an enduring and fruitful relationship that serves to educate both the hospice staff about important faith issues and the local faith communities about the excellent work carried out at Demelza House.

Promoting good community relations

Most local inter faith groups understand their overall work as promoting good community relations. In some cases, alongside their explicitly inter faith work, they have developed close working relationships with their local Race Equality Coucil. Local Race Equality Councils focus, as their name suggests, on the promotion of good race relations in their area. This reflects the statutory duty of the Commission for Racial Equality at UK level. However, to the extent that the Race Relations Act covers Jews and Sikhs as 'ethnic' groups and that many ethnic groups also self-define by overlapping religious identities, local RECs do sometimes support or become directly involved in inter faith work. Some, such as Kirklees REC, have been undertaking some significant work in this area, with the support of local inter faith bodies. It is important to be in touch with your local REC to let them know of the work of the inter faith body and also to find out if the REC is engaged in work which may be of interest.

Interfaith Kirklees was launched in 2005. The project is overseen by Kirklees Racial Equality Council, with project partners Kirklees SACRE, North Kirklees Interfaith Council, Huddersfield Interfaith Council, faith communities across Kirklees, Kirklees Metropolitan Council and the Government Office for Yorkshire and Humber.

It involves the development of seven 'faith centres' where school children actively engage with the faith of the community at that place of worship: Minster Church of All Saints, Dewsbury; Huddersfield Parish Church; the Hindu Society of Kirklees and Calderdale, Huddersfield; Masjid-e-Noor, Batley; Hanfia Institute, Huddersfield; Vajrapani Buddhist Centre, Huddersfield; and a Sikh faith centre involving the Shri Guru Singh Sabha Sikh Temple and Guru Nanak Sikh Sangat Temple in Huddersfield. At each centre, students find artefacts, displays and on-line facilities. Trained guides from the faith community are there to welcome pupils and support them through an interactive experience using packages designed by practising teachers and other professionals within the community. The project is not just for students – the centres are places for Kirklees residents to find out more about the faith of their neighbours.

The proposed new Commission on Equality and Human Rights (CEHR) will deal with various aspects of discrimination and equality including those relating to both race and 'religion and belief'. The new Commission is intended to have an important role in the promotion of 'good relations'. This will require consideration of how RECs and other bodies at regional and local level, such as local inter faith groups, which contribute to work on 'good relations' should relate to each other in this new context.

Some local inter faith bodies take an active part in equality and diversity work within their local authority area. Leicester Council of Faiths, for example, represents 'Faith and Belief' on the Leicester Equality and Diversity Partnership.

Acts and statements of solidarity

As part of their role in encouraging good community relations, local inter faith bodies have from time to time arranged special vigils, meetings and events or made short statements to witness to solidarity between people of different faiths at times of particular difficulty and potential tension, such as in the wake of the London bombings in July 2005.[4]

In Oldham, 'Standing Together', an event organised by the Council and **Oldham Inter Faith Forum**, brought the communities there together in Alexandra Park on 22 July to remember the victims of the London bombings; to show support for the emergency services; and to commit themselves to work together, across the communities of Oldham, to build respect and understanding and overcome the divisions and hatred which lead to such atrocities. Speakers included representatives of the Christian, Hindu, Jewish, and Muslim faiths and the Leader of the Council.

"We are united in deploring the use of murderous violence to achieve political or religious ends. We are most strongly distressed when perpetrators of violence claim they are serving God in this way. Such actions are no part of an honest observance of any of our faiths…" part of a statement by *Merseyside Council of Faiths*

"…We praise the prompt actions of the national police in searching for the truth, and, at a local level, the high level of consultation that we have received from local police leaders. We pledge our full support to them in ensuring community harmony in these coming days when all need to remain calm and focused in maintaining Leicester's reputation for good relations. As after 9/11, we affirm our declaration that faith leaders will consider any attack or act of vandalism against any religious building or individual connected with that community, as an attack on all of us."
Part of a statement by *Leicester Council of Faiths*

Inter faith initiatives in areas of limited religious diversity

There are some areas where religious diversity is relatively limited but where initiatives have been begun by individuals keen to foster greater inter faith awareness and understanding. West Somerset Interfaith Group and Shetland Inter Faith Group are just two examples of these sorts of initiatives which have an important role to play within the wider framework of national life.

Organisers of such groups often ensure a wide-ranging programme by:

● inviting speakers/visitors from more multi faith areas

● setting up a special 'twinning' link with a group in a more diverse area

● arranging occasional visits to places of worship in other parts of the country

● planning an annual exchange visit with a group from an area with a different religious make up, perhaps involving an overnight stay with each other's families

Subscribing to papers or journals of the various faith communities can be helpful as a way to be aware of issues of concern and as a basis for choosing topics for discussion.

Groups in less diverse areas often play a very important role in helping local schools broaden their understanding of inter religious issues.

West Somerset

We have established in the last two years a very good relationship with the Muslim community in Exeter. Following a visit by our group to them, we were hosts to quite a large group of them to an all day event here, where we were able to make use of a huge house for a day of shared worship, meal, discussion and talks. We also have an ongoing relationship with one of the Sikh gurdwaras in Bristol and have exchanged visits.

West Somerset Interfaith Group

Shetland

Although Shetland is limited in the diversity of faiths represented there, the Shetland Inter Faith Group keeps in touch with inter faith initiatives from more diverse areas of Scotland and, through its meetings, is raising awareness about different faiths in Scotland and around the world. The group held a video evening where the film 'The Message' which explores the life of the Prophet Muhammad (pbuh) was featured. At a later meeting they held a showing at the Islesburgh Community Centre, Lerwick of the ISEC film 'Ancient Futures: Learning from Ladakh' which showed much of the traditional life of the people of Ladakh and their high degree of cooperation and wisdom. The film explored the many challenges to traditional community life that the introduction of modern western ideas and values has brought.

Shetland Inter Faith Group

---

1 *The Bolton Faith Trail*, Bolton Inter Faith Council with Mike Cresswell, colour booklet published 2005 by Bolton Interfaith Council with support from Bolton Evening News, Bolton Community Network, Bolton Metropolitan Borough Council and the Church of England Diocese of Manchester. *Liverpool Walk of Faith*, Liverpool Hope College and Liverpool City Council, 2003, includes a map of the Liverpool walk and details of the 16 places of worship on it. It can be downloaded at www.liverpool.gov.uk.

2   Some perspectives of different faiths on involvement in shared events which may involve prayer or worship are outlined in *Working Together: Cooperation between Government and Faith Communities*, Home Office, 2004, pp 45-60.

3   See also Chapter 14 of the present guide on working in partnership with local authorities, LSPs and other public bodies.

4   Shortly after the bombings, the Inter Faith Network for the UK issued a document, *Looking After One Another: The Safety and Security of Our Faith Communities*. This gives practical guidelines for faith communities to respond jointly to such problems as attacks on their places of worship. The text of the document can be downloaded from **www.interfaith.org.uk**.

9 | Membership and structures

There are a number of bodies which give help and advice to voluntary organisations on such matters as finance, fund raising, committee structures, and volunteering, and you may wish to discuss with the local Council for Voluntary Service (CVS) the possibility of training in particular areas such as fund raising and effective use of resources. Often, however, a well written book exists which covers the topics your group or council may need to address.

Particularly useful when setting up a new organisation are the first two chapters of the publication *Voluntary But Not Amateur* by Ruth Hayes and Jacki Reason. These discuss the relative advantages of different organisational structures, the contents of a constitution and the arguments for and against seeking charitable status and incorporation. A more detailed guide to a wide range of legal issues is *The Voluntary Sector Legal Handbook* by Sandy Adirondack and James Sinclair Taylor (see under Resources: Publications for further details of these two books).

Membership

Some local inter faith organisations, like Leeds Faiths Forum (see pp17-18) are set up purely on an organisational membership basis while working in complementary fashion with other local bodies which involve individuals. The majority of local inter faith initiatives, however, are open to individual membership.[1] It is helpful, if possible, also to have faith community organisations, such as places of worship, in membership as this roots the initiative firmly in the day to day life of the local community.

Some councils explicitly list the religions they link, often some or all of the world religious traditions with significant communities in the UK and linked directly by the Inter Faith Network: Baha'i; Buddhist; Christian; Hindu; Jain; Jewish; Muslim; Sikh; and Zoroastrian. Other councils have organisational affiliation only from these nine faith communities, but have individual membership and attendance from other groups at 'open forum' events. The distinction between organisational and individual membership can be very important in this regard. Some inter faith councils have broader representation and in a few cases, there is a completely open door policy on admission. The Network's directory *Inter Faith Organisations in the UK* gives the current patterns of membership of all local groups listed in it (see under Resources: Publications).

There may be pressure for an inter faith organisation to admit, in the interest of inclusivity, groups whose admission would be divisive and could therefore disrupt the work of the body. In that case the organisation needs to balance these considerations and reach its own judgment on the right course to follow in order to achieve its own aims without compromising its integrity. As an independent body, a local inter faith organisation has to decide such matters for itself.

It is obviously important for a body which claims to be representative of local faith communities to have a sufficient range of membership to support that claim. In many ways the task of ensuring that a particular faith tradition is represented appropriately can be more taxing than dealing with the issue of which traditions should be included. Within each major tradition there are different groupings, sometimes based on different theological understandings and traditions and sometimes on different geographical origins overseas for a particular part of a community. The term 'faith community' itself can mask the fact that it may be composed of different 'communities'. There is also a need to consider how best to take advantage of 'umbrella' groups within particular communities, for example a local council of mosques or a local Churches Together grouping, while recognising that these groups might need to be supplemented if their coverage of a particular faith community is only partial.

Inter faith meetings can quite legitimately be of interest to those who are 'seeking' or who are on the margins of their own faith tradition. However, if a local inter faith organisation does not have a broadly based membership drawn from the main faith communities in its area (and if its pattern of officers does not reflect this), there is a risk that it will have a marginal feel which may put off potential attenders from those faith communities. In the case of a 'representative' body it is crucially important to ensure that mainstream involvement is maintained. If the main faith communities feel that the inter faith group or council is developing a 'marginal' feel they may remove their support for it. It is therefore highly desirable to proceed as far as possible by consensus in dealing with any membership issues which are controversial. It is also important to bear in mind the impact of membership decisions on the external profile of the organisations.

Whatever policy is adopted, the criteria for admission or involvement need to be discussed very carefully, made very clear, and reviewed from time to time.

Q: Just recently, we have had a membership application from a group some see as a 'new religious movement' and we are unclear whether to admit it. Is there any advice on this?

A: There are a number of quite sensitive issues involved in making decisions of this kind. The general impulse to be inclusive and welcoming is a positive one. However, members may have some genuine concerns about little known or recently formed religious groups (sometimes known by the pejorative term 'cults' but more appropriately termed 'new religious movements', or 'NRMs'). NRMs can see participation in inter faith groups and organisations as a path to public legitimacy and some can be quite forceful in their offers of assistance and involvement. A number of local inter faith groups have commented on the difficulty of knowing how to respond politely, in this context, to frequent kind offers of a group's premises or of catering for events. It is, however, very important that inter faith groups and councils rotate their venues or use neutral venues so as not to become publicly identified with a particular faith group, especially if it is a newer one and something of an unknown quantity.

If you are approached by a group of this kind (or indeed any unknown group or tradition) try to find out as much as you can before deciding how to respond. The organisation INFORM gives information and advice of a non-judgmental kind on NRMs (see under Resources: Organisations on page 105).

When thinking about issues of formal membership of your inter faith body by an NRM, it is important – as with all membership applications – to take into account whether their admission would enhance or adversely affect mainstream involvement in the work of your organisation.

Taking a considered position on a particular religious group does not, of course, imply any judgment on the personal integrity of an individual member of that group.

Steering groups, committees and officers

Some local inter faith groups operate quite happily with a relatively informal steering group which meets from time to time to consider the forward programme. For councils and forums with a wide programme of activities and a civic role an organising committee rapidly becomes vital.

It is important for multi faith bodies to reflect their diversity in their committees so that there is genuine shared ownership of the project. This is one of the reasons, among others, that increasing numbers of local inter faith bodies are developing constitutions which build in a requirement to include on the committee representatives of the main faiths in the area.

Many local inter faith bodies opt to have a structure with a chair, vice chair (or vice chairs), secretary, and an honorary treasurer. Some also opt to have a publicity officer or communications officer. There is usually a fixed term for which the posts can be held. It is important that the pattern of officers reflects reasonably well the multi faith nature of a body.

Q: Two individuals are both claiming to be the official representative of a particular community. How do we resolve this embarrassing situation?

A: Such a situation is not common, but it can occur in situations such as, for example, when there are several places of worship of a particular faith community and there is disagreement about the process for nominating their representatives. Such disagreements cannot always be avoided but the likelihood of them occurring can be lessened by having very clear guidelines about how each faith community puts forward names for the council of faiths, ensuring there are enough seats to allow for broad based representation and saying whether this is for a fixed or open-ended term. Make it clear that the seat on the council does not need to be filled by the most senior member of any faith, but rather by the person who can best serve the inter faith body and their faith community at any given time.

A problem can also occur if there has been a changeover of personnel on a management committee of a place of worship and the outgoing member does not want to relinquish his or her role. In very rare situations there can be difficulty because a faith community leader leaves his or her position with a faith community organisation or place of worship but still wants to carry on his or her inter faith role. In both of these types of situation the guiding principle should usually be that the currently recommended nominee from the place of worship or from the religion in question is the correct one. It can damage the credibility of inter faith relations to have on a committee, in a public role, an individual who is no longer an appropriate representative in the eyes of their community.

Constitutions and statements of aims

When initiatives become more formal, there is a need to articulate the aims and objectives clearly. Some groups and councils just have a simple 'statement of aims'. Others, as just noted above, have adopted constitutions. It is particularly important for organisations which are 'representative' in nature to have a constitution.

The Inter Faith Network can provide sample constitutions and give the addresses of local groups or councils in your region which can share their experiences. Local groups and councils often find it helpful to adopt formally the principles outlined in the short Inter Faith Network document, *Building Good Relations with People of Different Faiths and Beliefs* (reproduced at Annex B at the end of this guide).

Sometimes people worry that this is all 'boring bureaucracy' which will stifle their project. Unnecessary complexity should certainly be avoided, but the process of agreeing and writing down the group's aims and procedures is very important for groups with multi faith membership because it is part of operating with care and respect for each other's views. The discussion process actually has the potential to foster greater understanding and, if carried out well, it will actually contribute to the development of relationships of trust.

Constitutions need to cover such matters as:

- aims of the organisation (often called 'objects')
- powers, ie what the organisation can do to achieve its objects
- membership eligibility (organisational, individual or both)
- procedures for AGMs and for other meetings of members
- rights and duties of members
- election or appointment of committee members and their duties
- appointment of office bearers such as chairperson and secretary
- arrangements for determining classes of membership and subscriptions
- procedures for constitutional amendment
- procedures for winding up the organisation and disposing of its assets

Constitutions, once agreed, need to be reviewed from time to time.

Registering as a charity

Virtually all inter faith organisations have as constitutional objects (aims or purposes) 'the promotion of good inter faith relations' and other objects that are legally accepted as being charitable purposes. If all of the organisation's objects are legally charitable, and it is based in England or Wales, and its annual income from all sources is more than £1,000, it is legally required to register with the Charity Commission. At the time of writing there are proposals to increase the registration threshold to £5,000. Charities based in Scotland must register with the Office of the Scottish Charity Regulator (OSCR).

Registration as a charity is not in itself a difficult process. However the registration authorities will require the organisation to have a proper constitution, and a plan that shows the organisation is likely to be viable.

Advice on registration for charities based in England and Wales, including model constitutions, is available from the Charity Commission, Harmsworth House, Bouverie Street, London EC4Y 8DP, tel 0845 3000 218, www.charitycommission.gov.uk. Charities in Scotland can get information from the Office of the Scottish Charity Regulator, Argyll House, Marketgait, Dundee DD1 1QP, tel 01382 220446, www.oscr.org.uk (this may change to www.oscr.gov.uk at some point). Charities in Northern Ireland currently do not register with a regulatory body, but get recognition of their charitable status through the Inland Revenue Charities Unit, St John's House, Merton Road, Bootle L69 9BB, tel 0845 302 0203, www.hmrc.gov.uk/charities

Incorporation

If a group or council has a significant financial turnover, plans to employ staff, or wants to lease or own property, then it may wish to consider incorporation as a company limited by guarantee as this affords greater liability protection to Trustees. However, most local inter faith organisations are unincorporated. Guidance on incorporation can be found in the London Voluntary Service Council publication *Voluntary But Not Amateur* (see under

Resources: Publications). Guidance on incorporation can be found in *Voluntary But Not Amateur* and *The Voluntary Sector Legal Handbook* (see under Resources: Publications), and in the Charity Commission's charity registration pack (see above). Advice may be available from local councils for voluntary service and similar voluntary sector support agencies.

It is important to be aware that the company form used for community organisations – the company limited by guarantee – is quite different from the company limited by shares form used for businesses. If using a legal adviser, it is important to get appropriate advice.

---

1   *Local Inter Faith Activity: A Survey*, Inter Faith Network, 2003, p 17, 90% of groups responding had individual members.

10 | Money matters

Local inter faith groups, like faith communities, are an amazing example of volunteer power! Most run solely on the goodwill and energy of commited people. Increasingly, however, the growing level of interest in inter faith issues is generating a level of activity which requires more servicing and more support than in the past.

Financial matters and funding

Banking and handling of financial matters

If a group or council organises events or activities it is likely to have income and expenditure to manage. It is helpful to have an honorary treasurer, and the constitution may require this. Unless the organisation deals only with very small amounts of money, it should open its own bank or building society account. The committee should agree:

- what sort of account is most appropriate for the organisation and where it should be held

- appropriate rules for recording income and expenditure, in particular showing that grants or donations received for a specific purpose ('restricted funds') are used for that purpose

- who may sign cheques and how many signatures are needed

- what expenses will be reimbursed and what procedure must be followed for claims

- where any remaining funds or other assets will go in the event of the group being dissolved (for example to the nearest local inter faith initiative)

Most major banks and building societies produce short guidelines for small organisations wanting to open accounts and you may find it helpful to ask at your local branches. In deciding what type of account to open and which bank to use, the committee should consider whether some types of accounts might be more acceptable than others to some members of the organisation.

Sources of funding

There will be a need to decide how the organisation's activities are to be financed. The main options are membership fees and funding from trusts, local authorities and/or the Big Lottery Fund. Grant money usually brings with it extra requirements to monitor and evaluate work. It is important to be clear who, within your local inter faith body, is responsible for ensuring this happens. It also is important to ensure that the terms and conditions of a grant do not unduly erode a body's independence.

Membership fees Most local inter faith bodies have annual membership fees. Some have two types of fees: individual and organisational, with two corresponding levels of subscription. Individual membership fees tend to be between £5 and £10 and organisational fees vary between £20 and £100.

Trusts Some local inter faith organisations are able to secure grants from trusts. The Directory of Social Change publishes a useful series of guides to grant making trusts (see under Resources: Publications for further details).

Local authorities In some areas, local authorities are supporting local inter faith initiatives through grants, through making premises available or through 'in kind' support with local authority staff helping service meetings or events or mailings being done for the local inter faith body. Detailed examples are given in *Local Inter Faith Activity in the UK: A Survey*.[1]

In the context of funding from the local authority or other public bodies, it is important to know about 'Compacts'. Local Compacts provide the framework for partnership working between local public sector bodies, such as local authorities and Local Strategic Partnerships, and local voluntary and community sector organisations. Nearly all local authorities have, or are in the process of developing, a 'compact' with their local voluntary and community sector. These local 'compacts' take account of a national framework document which was published in 1998.[2] That document was subsequently supplemented by five Codes of Good Practice on: Funding; Consultation and Policy Appraisal; Black and Minority Ethnic Communities; Volunteering; and

Community Groups. The original *Compact Code of Good Practice on Funding*, which was launched in 2000, was revised and updated in 2005 as the *Funding and Procurement Compact Code of Good Practice*.[3]

The Compact Mediation Scheme, which provides an independent service to resolve disputes that arise in relationships under the Compact, was extended in 2004 to cover disputes relating to Local Compacts.

Leicester

In 1986, members of different faith communities in Leicester met at the town hall at the initiative of the Lord Mayor and went on to form themselves into a council of faiths. **Leicester Council of Faiths**' members represent, on a faith community basis, the eight principal faiths in the City: Baha'is, Buddhists, Christians, Hindus, Jains, Jews, Muslims and Sikhs. There are also 10 further nominated members with specialist knowledge in areas such as RE.

Leicester Council of Faiths has retained a strong link with Leicester City Council. It is consulted by the Council on a range of issues from education to neighbourhood renewal and community strategy. The Council provides funding, via the Education Department, towards the rent of LCF's Welcome Centre, some running costs, and the salary of a part-time coordinator.

This is one of the sources which enables LCF to carry out a wide programme of work to promote good inter faith relations in Leicester, including events, publications (such as the directory of places of worship in Leicester), faiths awareness training, and assistance to a wide range of bodies such as the police, schools, universities, hospitals and the fire and rescue service. It also supports, with other partners, Leicester's Faiths Regeneration Officer.

Lottery funding Lottery money has become a source of funding for many charities. However, if your body is considering applying for support from lottery sources, it is important to discuss the matter with members to ensure that they are content with this and that there is consensus about any such application. The reason for this is that some faith traditions, notably Islam and some strands of the Christian tradition, do not approve of gambling and may not wish funds to come from this source.

Other

From time to time there are opportunities for local inter faith organisations to apply for grants under central Government funding programmes. The most recent example of this is the Faith Communities Capacity Building Fund, for which the Home Office invited applications to be made during the Autumn of 2005.[4] So far, such funding schemes have been for time-limited projects or programmes of work.

1 *Local Inter Faith Activity in the UK: A Survey,* Inter Faith Network, 2003, pp 29-30; 34-35; and 78-80.

2 *Compact: Getting it Right Together (Compact on Relations between Government and the Voluntary and Community Sector in England).* Home Office 1998.

3 All the Compact codes of good practice can be downloaded free from: www.homeoffice.gov.uk/comrace/active/compact/publications.html.

4 Fund administered for the Home Office by the Community Development Foundation.

11 | Volunteers, employees and premises

Volunteers

The majority of local inter faith bodies are established and run wholly on a voluntary basis. That is to say, those involved give their time and skills with no payment and are therefore volunteers even if they would not normally think of that term in relation to their work. It can be helpful, however, to remember that a body is receiving this gift and for there to be occasions where people are thanked for what they do.

Employees

A few local inter faith bodies employ at least a part time worker to help respond to the growing number of requests for involvement from local authorities, Local Strategic Partnerships, schools, hospitals, police, fire service and other bodies. Some local inter faith bodies have a full or part time staff member to help with their programme.[1]

Where there are paid workers careful thought needs to be given to how they will be recruited and how their work will be managed and supported and how their role will be defined in relation to the kinds of activities carried out by committee members in a voluntary capacity.

To recruit and take on staff is to take on significant legal responsibilities. It is important to be aware of these and to ensure that any committee is aware of its obligations and liabilities.[2]

Local inter faith bodies employing staff must also ensure that they comply with legislation dealing with discrimination on grounds of race, gender, disability, sexual orientation, religion or belief, and (from October 2006) age. Employers, including religious organisations, are prohibited from treating an employee or potential employee less (or more) favourably on the basis of religion or belief. There are, however, exceptions where being of a particular religion can be shown to be a 'genuine and determining occupational requirement' for the job or is necessary to preserve an organisation's 'ethos' where this is based on religion or belief.

Premises

Most local inter faith bodies do not have their own premises. A few, however, have secured a small office or a welcome centre and find this creates a higher profile and a greater ability to develop a programme useful to people in their area. If your body chooses to do this, it is important to obtain information about the legal aspects of owning or leasing premises.[3]

If the organisation does not have its own premises but occupies a corner in another organisation's premises, it is generally helpful to write down the arrangements. These could include, for example, use of photocopiers and other equipment, contributing towards the cost of electricity, and similar matters. Informal arrangements that work well at the beginning can become problematic later on if they are not in writing.

Insurance

The types of insurance cover needed for inter faith organisations and the events they hold vary according to such factors as whether they employ staff, or own or lease premises. If the body employs staff, even on a part-time basis, there is a statutory obligation to take out employer's liability insurance. If it has premises and/or holds events, it may need public liability insurance. Contents and/or buildings insurance may be appropriate.

The Charity Commission produces a short guidance publication: CC49 – Charities and Insurance which can be ordered from the Commission or found at www.charity-commission.gov.uk/publications/cc49.asp#4

---

1 *Inter Faith Organisations in the UK: A Directory,* Second Edition, Inter Faith Network, 2005 includes information about the staff numbers of all local bodies listed in it.

2 See the publications *Voluntary But Not Amateur: A Guide to the Law for Voluntary Organisations and Community Groups,* Ruth Hayes and Jacki Reason, LVSC, 2004 and *The Voluntary Sector Legal Handbook* Sandy Adirondack and James Sinclair Taylor, Directory of Social Change, 2001.

3 See *Voluntary But Not Amateur* and *The Voluntary Sector Legal Handbook.*

12 | Making your work known

Local inter faith bodies have a positive story to tell. It is important to tell it widely and well.

The media

90% of people read a local paper and 50% of people listen to a local radio station. Local media can help give a higher profile to your events and projects. They are also an important arena for your group to contribute to improving community relations through rebutting negative images and stereotypes of religious people or groups and letting local people know about the ways that people of different faiths are working together.

If possible, designate someone to be responsible for being the media contact. Build and keep up to date a short media list with the names and contact details of local journalists and editors. Send clearly written media releases in advance of events you hope to publicise.

The Media Trust, which is a charity which works with the voluntary sector, produces short and helpful on-line guides to all aspects of working with the media. You can find these at www.mediatrust.org. It is also the base for the Community Channel, a national digital television channel which is "dedicated to inspiring people to do more with their lives" and covers news from community groups such as local inter faith bodies. You can let them know about your events or projects by emailing them at info@communitychannel.org.

Some inter faith groups and councils are already successfully getting coverage in their local media. For example, in Newcastle upon Tyne and Gateshead, inter faith group members met with the editor of *The Journal*, Tyneside's local paper, and their conversations have resulted in the regular publishing of a 16 page supplement entitled 'Living Together'. Interfaith Milton Keynes has an ongoing relationship with the local press. Every month an article for the *Sunday Citizen* is written and different members take it in turn to write the articles. The 'Three Counties Inter Faith Group'[1] contributes once a month on a Sunday to a radio slot ('Melting Pot') on Three Counties Radio. In each slot there are three different speakers, each from a different religion and from a different county of the three counties. So, for example a progamme on marriage included a Baha'i from Bedfordshire, a Hindu from Buckinghamshire and a Christian from Hertfordshire.

Making statements on current issues

According to the recent survey of local inter faith groups, less than half make statements on current issues. Some groups and councils prefer to avoid any statements except for broad statements about the underlying need to work constructively together. However, it may be that your group or council feels called to make a statement on a matter of local concern or on a national or international issue which is having a major impact on local inter faith relations. A statement by a 'representative' council is naturally likely to carry more weight than one from an informal group.

It is vital that any public statements by a council or group do properly reflect views within it, or it will become discredited. Where statements are made, consensus is of great importance. If a public statement of policy or views is agreed only by a narrow margin, it is unlikely to be supported by the defeated minority. If general agreement cannot be reached on a matter, it may be preferable to leave it to the individual faith communities to make their views known as they wish, following the opportunity to hear the views of others in the course of the discussion on the issue. It may not be necessary to take a position, but rather simply to state a shared concern and suggest some principles for consideration.

If it is decided that a statement is desirable, it is helpful to ensure that it is properly publicised. In addition to the Media Trust resources mentioned above a useful publication is Directory of Social Change's, *DIY Guide to Public Relations* by Moi Ali (see under Resources: Publications).

Speaking to the media

A number of local inter faith organisations have developed protocols to guide their members on procedures for dealing with the media. A protocol covers such points as who may speak on behalf of the local inter faith body and what procedure should be followed in response to media enquiries. It can help ensure that if individuals are approached by the press or others to comment on issues or events locally or further afield they avoid being drawn into offering statements on behalf of the inter faith body without proper collective authorisation for these.

Newsletters

Many local inter faith councils and groups have a newsletter which goes out to members regularly. These are usually short and simple and let members know about forthcoming events. If there are articles about aspects of particular faiths, there is a need to ensure that different faiths are given roughly similar space over the course of the year. Some groups include in their newsletter a short list of the different faiths' festivals in the period ahead.

Newsletters can be created fairly easily on a computer. Easy to read print is important and a reasonably large font size (11 point or larger) with lots of white space between items helps most readers.

Websites

Increasingly, local inter faith bodies are developing their own websites. These are a reasonably cheap and highly effective way to let people know what you are doing.

> **Some examples of local inter faith body websites are:**
>
> **www.bcof.org.uk** Bedford Council of Faiths
>
> **www.ifcg.co.uk** Brighton and Hove Interfaith Contact Group
>
> **www.cam.net.uk/home/interfaith** Cambridge Inter-Faith Group
>
> **difa.port5.com** Dundee Inter Faith Association
>
> **www.harrowinterfaith.org.uk** Harrow Inter Faith Council
>
> **www.leicestercounciloffaiths.org.uk** Leicester Council of Faiths
>
> **www.interfaithnottm.org.uk** Nottingham Inter Faith Council
>
> **www.readinginterfaith.co.uk** Reading Interfaith Group
>
> **www.southampton-faiths.org** Southampton Inter Faith Link and Southampton Council of Faiths
>
> **www.sifre.org.uk** Suffolk Inter-Faith Resource

1   Inter faith groups in Bedfordshire, Buckinghamshire and Hertfordshire have formed the Three Counties Interfaith Network for mutual support and sharing of information and good practice.

13 | Keeping a good thing going

In the early days of a new initiative high levels of energy help start the ball rolling. People are enthusiastic and make an extra effort to come to meetings and get the right people involved. But it is important to plan for the long term.

Maintaining a strong pattern of involvement

Often a lot of leg work is done when councils and groups are set up. Visits are carried out, calls made and letters written. Then an initiative gets under way and everyone wants to focus on content and not to have to keep checking on participation. But the checking and the updating are essential. It is useful to have at least two contacts for each group in case people suddenly leave or go away for a long time.

Some groups and councils have a regular schedule by which each year the chair, secretary or another designated person makes fact finding calls to see if new people from the various religious organisations may now need to be drawn into the work. It is particularly important for representative councils of faiths that their contacts are up to date. People may be able to give very valuable input in their individual capacity, but on a council's committee the people in the public eye need to be those officially recognised by their religious organisation or place of worship.

Sometimes members of some faith traditions seem more enthusiastic than others. A group might find, for example, that, over the years, it has become primarily Christian or that it has a high number of Baha'is or Hindus by comparison with, say, Sikhs in relation to the general population balance in the area. When a group becomes noticeably imbalanced, this can make the problem even worse. The occasional Sikh – to continue the example – who comes to the group may feel it is not really for him or her, and will not feel inclined to stay. For this reason it is necessary that, if imbalance seems to be developing, the group decides on a remedy.

Making fresh contact with every local faith community and speaking in person with a key person or persons is particularly important in such a situation. It may be helpful to ask straightforward questions about why people are not attending. Often the cause is that involvement in the local group does not seem an especially high priority. If this is the case, it is useful to discover why that might be. The group may want to make some changes to remedy the situation.

> This year we carried out a 'SWOT' analysis, looking at **Bolton Interfaith Council**'s strengths, weaknesses, opportunities and threats. It helped us think about responding to perceived weaknesses and threats, such as lack of a regular meeting place, inadequate funding, low involvement of women of different faiths, overstretched personnel and resources and poor levels of attendance at some meetings. It also, very importantly, reminded us of many strengths of BIC such as the range of faiths involved in our work, our commitment to a common vision and our high level of recognition locally and it helped us think about important opportunities like the possibility of reaching out into local government, creating local forums around the Borough, developing a list of speakers for briefings and talks, engaging with young people, and working in partnership with other local organisations like Bolton College and Bolton University.

Reviewing your aims and objectives from time to time

Sometimes groups which have been in existence for some years find that there is a genuine difference of opinion among members about whether they should evolve in a different direction, for example moving from an informal and 'fellowship' aspect towards a more representative 'council' pattern. It may be helpful to initiate a review which asks such questions as: Is our group or council still of the kind best for our area? Do we still have the same aims and objectives? Can we develop ways to involve more people – especially active members of the major local faith communities? How can we respond in our programme to the needs of both established and new members? If members of the group have time to visit local faith communities and other bodies, such as the local authority, which may have views on the work of the local inter faith group, this fact finding will prove very helpful.

Q: Some of our members seem to be very comfortable with the little circle of participants who have belonged to the group for years and seem actively to discourage attempts to bring in more people, especially people who may be more conservative religiously than them. Is this a common situation?

A: It can occasionally happen that people of different faith traditions who share a particular outlook find they have more in common with each other than they do with people of their own faith tradition who are either more liberal or more conservative than they are. Sometimes a group can become a comfortable place for them and they are reluctant to change settled ways. This is not a problem if the group is a private one for individuals who have become friends, but it is problematic in towns and cities where no alternative inter faith initiative exists and where getting all the major faiths involved is vital. Try gradually getting the group to invite more challenging speakers and perhaps invite a speaker from one of the national inter faith organisations to give a talk about why it can be helpful to widen the circle of dialogue.

Keeping sight of the importance of the initiative

There will be times when an initiative may seem hard to sustain. Perhaps funding has dwindled or enthusiasm has waned. Or there may be international difficulties which are making local inter faith relations more tense than usual.

It can sometimes feel a tough challenge to remember all the good that a local inter faith body has accomplished and to keep a positive forward momentum. Inter faith work is not always easy and it sometimes seems undervalued in the public eye. But it remains immensely important. It is a key factor that is helping our society develop in a harmonious and respectful way.

14 | Working with local authorities, Local Strategic Partnerships and regional structures

The local authority

In Chapter 5 a number of examples were given of the work of local inter faith organisations with local authorities, as well as other public bodies.

It is helpful to develop a good working relationship with your local authority. Some local authorities now have a staff member and/or a councillor with a special responsibility for faith and inter faith issues. Find out who this is and arrange to talk with them about your initiative and to find out about potential areas of common interest and action.

Local authorities now have a very direct involvement in inter faith matters for two reasons:

- Their statutory duties in a number of areas require them to consult with faith communities and they often like to do so at one shared table, hence their interest in multi faith consultation mechanisms.

- They are working to deepen community cohesion and inter faith organisations can play a major role in this.

Greater detail about the legislative and regulatory factors which have contributed to increased local inter faith activity by local authorities and other public bodies will be found in *Local Inter Faith Activity in the UK: A Survey*[1] and also in *Faith and Community: A Good Practice Guide for Local Authorities* (see under Resources: Publications). As noted in Chapter 2, local authorities have shown increased interest in helping set up or support local inter faith structures.

A proposal to set up a network of local authority officials with responsibility for faith issues was announced by the Government in January 2005.[2] It is called the Local Authority Faith

Communities Link. It is being developed by the Office of the Deputy Prime Minister in partnership with the Home Office and Government Offices for the Regions. It met for the first time in June 2005 and has two purposes:

● within government structures: to improve partnership and communication between central, regional and local government in working with faith communities.

● at the local level: to support local authorities and other public agencies in their work with local faith communities through sharing experience and good practice.

Further information about the Link can be obtained from the Office of the Deputy Prime Minister or the Cohesion and Faiths Unit of the Home Office (see under Resources: Organisations at the back of this guide). If your local authority is part of the Link, it will be particularly important to be in touch with its relevant official.

Local Strategic Partnerships

Local Strategic Partnerships (LSPs) bring different parts of the public sector together with the private, community and voluntary sectors to work together to ensure that public services meet the needs of local people. They prepare and implement a community strategy; bring together local plans, partnerships and initiatives; work with those local authorities that are developing public service agreements; and develop and deliver a neighbourhood renewal strategy. Since the introduction of Local Area Agreements in 2004, LSPs have had a key role in the application of resources through this new funding mechanism.[3]

LSPs are expected to make real efforts to involve people who are traditionally under-represented, such as faith communities and black and minority ethnic communities. Consequently, in multi faith areas, many will see the local inter faith body as a natural source for this. However, in areas where an inter faith body is not seen as representative of the main local faith communities or where it does not want to engage with the LSP, the LSP may develop, often through the Community Empowerment Network, a separate multi faith consultative forum.[4] Many LSPs have either one or two 'faith' places. In some areas, such as Northampton, the local inter faith body has been invited to nominate someone for the faith place on the LSP.

In February 2002 the first **Wandsworth Faith Communities Meeting** was held. Representatives from the main faith communities in the borough, identified through the Census, were invited to meet with the Leader of the Council and the Chief Executive.

The aim of the meeting was:

- to update and inform representatives about important developments such as the Local Strategic Partnership (LSP)

- to develop the group's links to the LSP and hence provide a voice for faith communities into it

- to explain the various consultation exercises planned where faith communities' input would be helpful

- to discuss any issues of mutual interest

- to provide an opportunity to resolve potential concerns or tensions quickly and effectively.

The WFCM is now a formal sub-group of the Local Strategic Partnership. It meets on a quarterly basis and has organised two multi faith seminars that have each been attended by over 100 representatives of the local community.

Dudley Interfaith Network is a member of **Dosti**, the Community Empowerment Network for the Borough of Dudley, which is in turn the vehicle for voluntary and community sector representation on our Local Strategic Partnership. As an element of this we are working with three other Dosti networks (Dudley Race Equality Council, Dudley Muslim Forum and Dudley Borough Churches Forum), and on behalf of the LSP, to address community cohesion issues that relate specifically to race and faith.

Other local partnerships

There will be a range of LSP sub-partnerships as well as independent partnerships dealing with such issues as neighbourhood renewal and regeneration. If you are in touch with your LSP, you will be likely to hear about these as a matter of course and there is the potential for direct involvement. A helpful resource for local inter faith bodies which are interested in regeneration issues is the Faith-based Regeneration Network (see Resources: Organisations).

Regional structures

It is helpful for local inter faith bodies to be in contact with their regional faith forum if there is one. There are now regional faith forums in six of the English Regions and forums are likely to be launched in the near future in two other Regions.[5] The sorts of functions they carry out vary but include:

- acting as a consultative forum for regional government

- acting as the nominating body for the faiths seat on the Regional Assembly and its panels

- holding regular dialogue with, and submitting position statements to, the Regional Assembly, Regional Development Agency, the Government Office and the voluntary sector at regional level

- making written submissions on regional consultation documents

- attending consultative meetings relating to regional issues

- sending representatives to serve on local government strategic initiatives

Local inter faith bodies may also wish to establish contact with the Government Offices for the Regions and also the Regional Development Agencies and the 'Regional Chambers' linked to them, some of which include specific places allocated for faith sector representatives. The Inner Cities Religious Council Secretariat (see under Resources: Organisations) can provide contact details.

Anxieties about partnership

"In some ways, local authorities and local inter faith groups and councils are like strangers who have barely met before they are asked to step out to the dance floor and waltz. There is anxiety about a little known partner, puzzlement about who leads and worry about how the performance will be judged. Both sides have reasons for caution and, although there is genuine and important common ground, the separate agendas do not overlap 100% so it is perhaps unsurprising that there is anxiety about how to negotiate differences."[6]

Sometimes there are those within faith communities who feel somewhat ambivalent about engagement with a local authority or other public bodies. Their reservations may be linked partly to a concern about the risk of cooption to a 'political' agenda and partly to worry about the time which such work it can consume. This is not surprising but, on the other hand, without engagement faith communities cannot take advantage of the opportunities which have markedly expanded in recent years for them to play a greater role in contributing to issues of concern to their local areas and to work in partnership with others for the common good.

Although the involvement of local authorities can be helpful, the most important factor in ensuring a sustainable local inter faith initiative is a genuine desire on the part of different local faith communities to develop deeper relationships between their members and to work cooperatively.

Those within local authorities and other public bodies can have their own anxieties about partnership working. For many, interacting with faith and inter faith bodies is a relatively new process and new ways of working have to be found.

Inter Faith Activity in the UK: A Survey (see under Resources: Publications) discusses in detail some of the issues which inter faith bodies and local authorities and other public bodies face when finding helpful ways to work in partnership. It is important to stress, however, that overall the relationship in most areas of the UK appears to be a positive and evolving one with both types of body gaining much from cooperation.

Southampton Council of Faiths (SCOF) grew out of the **Southampton Inter Faith Link** and has developed alongside this more informal body. SCOF came into being to address the growing need for faith representation in the city. It has built a strong relationship with the City Council, engaging with it on areas such as community cohesion and community tension and on specific issues such as appropriate burial arrangements for Muslims. Since 2003, it has provided the Mayor with 'faith advisers' from each of the seven faiths it links. It is a source of faith representation at events such as the Remembrance Sunday service and the marking of the 60th anniversary of VE and VJ days which are organised by the Mayor's Office for the City Council.

We arranged and hosted a major conference, 'Issues of Identity, Faith and Culture', for 150 people representing the faith communities of Suffolk and people working in the statutory bodies. As a result we were invited to deliver ongoing lunch-time seminars on the faiths for County Council staff in Ipswich and also for St Edmundsbury Borough Council. We have run a similar conference in Lowestoft in partnership with Waveney District Council and Lowestoft College, and have been asked to facilitate one in Bury St Edmunds. *Suffolk Inter-Faith Resource*

1 *Local Inter Faith Activity in the UK: A Survey*, Inter Faith Network, 2003, pp 140-143.

2 *Improving Opportunity, Strengthening Society: the Government's Strategy to increase Race Equality and Community Cohesion*, Home Office, 2005.

3 Further information about LSPs, designed specifically for community groups, is available on the website of the Urban Forum, www.urbanforum.org.uk. It includes a basic LSP guide which can be downloaded free of charge.

4 *Local Inter Faith Activity in the UK: A Survey* pp 141-143 gives further information about LSPs and their involvement in inter faith issues.

5 Contact details for regional faith forums can be found on the Network's website: www.interfaith.org.uk.

6 *Local Inter Faith Activity in the UK: A Survey*, p 106.

ANNEX A

Catering for multi faith events

Many groups have social gatherings where shared food and hospitality play an important part. A shared meal, announced as vegetarian, ensures that each community has some familiar food. Careful labelling of all dishes allows participants to explore new tastes without anxiety about accidentally eating foods not acceptable to them for religious reasons. It is a good idea to discuss food issues with your group or council and agree a basic set of guidelines.

If you are arranging an event which involves sharing of food, the following guidelines may be useful. It may be helpful to give a copy of them to the caterers for an event and have them available should anyone be interested to see them.

Generally speaking, the best way to cater for a multi faith event so that the maximum number of people can share in the food is to make it fully vegetarian, with some vegan options, and to label each dish.

Other pointers:

- Have some dishes which contain no eggs and ensure that some of these non-egg dishes also contain no garlic or onions (since all these may be unacceptable to some Hindus, observant Jains and also some other groupings).

- Devout Jains also avoid eating all root vegetables (such as potatoes) because they believe that ahimsa or nonviolence requires that you do not kill any plant: it is only acceptable to eat vegetables and fruits the removal of which leaves the plant itself alive. Consequently it can be useful to have one carefully labelled main dish or type of sandwich which contains not only no eggs, garlic or onions, but also no root vegetables.

- No animal fat should be used in any vegetarian cooking, and when cheese is used it should be of the kind labelled 'vegetarian' which indicates that it has not been made with rennet which comes from cows' stomachs.

- If making sandwiches, avoid any butter substitutes made with rendered beef fat. The label will indicate use of such fat – at least one butter substitute on the market does use this form of fat.

- Avoid the following e numbers as they are non-vegetarian: E120 Cochineal; E441 Gelatine; E542 Edible Bone Phosphate. Some other e number substances can also be produced from animal sources. A full list can be found at www.vegsoc.org/info/enumbers.html.

- Any biscuits provided should contain no animal fats other than butter, and preferably there should be some which also do not contain egg. Also check the label to ensure that cochineal has not been used in their production as this is not vegetarian.

- Puddings should not include gelatine (unless it is of a vegetarian variety).

- Alcohol should not be used in the preparation of any food.

- List ingredients, so that people with religious or health reasons to avoid particular foods can do so.

Within Judaism, the kosher rule is widely observed, but with differing interpretations. Check in advance how your Jewish participants interpret it. Normally, it is sufficient to provide totally vegetarian food and disposable plates, cups and cutlery. However, for the strictly Orthodox, it may be necessary to bring in separate meals which have been prepared in a kosher kitchen. Kosher foods include kosher wine, bread and cheese as well as meats. Such food and drink is marked with a hechsher (seal) which certifies it is kosher.

Muslims will wish that, ideally, their food has been prepared in a kitchen where the utensils and contents have not been in contact with haram (forbidden) food. However, most Muslims are primarily concerned to ensure that any meat served is halal (permitted and slaughtered in accordance with Islamic law), and are generally happy to eat vegetarian food that has no animal fat or by-products used in its production.

If meat and fish are used, it is wise to use chicken or turkey and to avoid food offensive to some religious groups, such as pork, beef, and also prawns (which, together with a number of other types of shellfish and fish, are non-kosher under Jewish dietary rules). It is important to spell out the issue in advance to any food preparers. Similarly, the point sometimes needs to be emphasised that fish products are not suitable for use in vegetarian meals.

If meat and/or fish dishes or sandwiches are provided as part of a meal, ensure that they are on separate plates from the vegetarian foods. Caterers are often unaware of the fact that sandwiches should not be mixed, and may mistakenly serve ham sandwiches on the same platter as vegetarian ones, or sausage rolls next to vegetarian snacks. If using an external caterer for an event, underline that any meat and fish items must be on completely separate platters.

Different traditions have varying approaches to the consumption of alcohol. In Islam it is forbidden and there are warnings against the dangers that can arise from associating with those who drink alcohol. Baha'is also do not drink alcohol and avoid the use of it in preparation of foods. For Hindus and Jains, it is considered undesirable. Sikhs who have received Amrit have committed themselves not to drink alcohol. For many Christians alcohol can be enjoyed in moderation as one of the gifts of creation. Some Christian groups, however, advocate abstinence. Within Judaism, there is no prohibition and responsible use of alcohol is not frowned upon. Practice varies among Buddhists, although alcohol is viewed as dangerous in so far as it can hinder 'mindfulness'. Because of the diversity of practice within religions, it is perhaps best not to serve alcohol at specifically inter faith events. If you do decide to provide alcohol at a function, set it at some distance from the nonalcoholic drinks (which should be clearly labelled). Fruit juice and mineral water should always be provided as alternatives.

Coffee and tea, as stimulants, are avoided by observant members of certain traditions. It is therefore important to provide juice, water or herbal tea as alternatives to morning and afternoon coffee and tea. Biscuits should be vegetarian, including some vegan ones, and be clearly labelled.

ANNEX B

Building Good Relations with People of Different Faiths and Beliefs

In Britain today, people of many different faiths and beliefs live side by side. The opportunity lies before us to work together to build a society rooted in the values we treasure. But this society can only be built on a sure foundation of mutual respect, openness and trust. This means finding ways to live our lives of faith with integrity, and allowing others to do so too. Our different religious traditions offer us many resources for this and teach us the importance of good relationships characterised by honesty, compassion and generosity of spirit. The Inter Faith Network offers the following code of conduct for encouraging and strengthening these relationships.

As members of the human family, we should show each other respect and courtesy. In our dealings with people of other faiths and beliefs this means exercising good will and:

- Respecting other people's freedom within the law to express their beliefs and convictions

- Learning to understand what others actually believe and value, and letting them express this in their own terms

- Respecting the convictions of others about food, dress and social etiquette and not behaving in ways which cause needless offence

- Recognising that all of us at times fall short of the ideals of our own traditions and never comparing our own ideals with other people's practices

- Working to prevent disagreement from leading to conflict

- Always seeking to avoid violence in our relationships

When we talk about matters of faith with one another, we need to do so with sensitivity, honesty and straightforwardness. This means:

- Recognising that listening as well as speaking is necessary for a genuine conversation

- Being honest about our beliefs and religious allegiances

- Not misrepresenting or disparaging other people's beliefs and practices

- Correcting misunderstanding or misrepresentations not only of our own but also of other faiths whenever we come across them

- Being straightforward about our intentions

- Accepting that in formal inter faith meetings there is a particular responsibility to ensure that the religious commitment of all those who are present will be respected

All of us want others to understand and respect our views. Some people will also want to persuade others to join their faith. In a multi faith society where this is permitted, the attempt should always be characterised by self-restraint and a concern for the other's freedom and dignity. This means:

- Respecting another person's expressed wish to be left alone

- Avoiding imposing ourselves and our views on individuals or communities who are in vulnerable situations in ways which exploit these

- Being sensitive and courteous

- Avoiding violent action or language, threats, manipulation, improper inducements, or the misuse of any kind of power

- Respecting the right of others to disagree with us

Living and working together is not always easy. Religion harnesses deep emotions which can sometimes take destructive forms. Where this happens, we must draw on our faith to bring about reconciliation and understanding. The truest fruits of religion are healing and positive. We have a great deal to learn from one another which can enrich us without undermining our own identities. Together, listening and responding with openness and respect, we can move forward to work in ways that acknowledge genuine differences but build on shared hopes and values.

© Inter Faith Network for the UK, 1993

ANNEX C

Talking religion

Although religion may not cause wars it can certainly lead to heated discussion! People often speak with passion. Here are a few points to keep in mind when speaking about faith and religious topics:

- When asking questions of others about their faith, offer a genuine, personal reason for your query

- Find out what others actually believe and value, and let them express this in their own terms – remember that there is diversity of practice and thought within each of the main religions

- Find out what you have in common; what connects you rather than divides you

- Respect the other person's right to express their beliefs and convictions and to disagree

- We are not all the same – accept and respect the fact that the religious beliefs of someone may affect what they eat, what they wear and many of the ways they deal with other people

- Ensure your faith is presented with integrity – be prepared to say 'I don't know the answer to that, but I'll find out'

- Take care that everyone understands the religious terms that you are using – ask, "Is this clear?" every so often

- A sense of humour is good, but take care – jokes on religious topics can cause offence

Background

These short guidelines were produced for youth inter faith discussion groups. They were published in *Connect: Different Faiths Shared Values,* Inter Faith Network in association with the National Youth Agency and TimeBank, 2004.

© Inter Faith Network, 2004

ANNEX D

The Shared Act of Reflection and Commitment by the Faith Communities of the UK

The Inter Faith Network was invited by the Government to assist the Department for Culture, Media and Sport in developing and organising, as part of the official Millennium celebrations, a Shared Act of Reflection and Commitment by the Faith Communities of the UK. This complemented the Millennium Church Services held in Belfast, Cardiff, Edinburgh and London.

This unprecedented event was held in the Royal Gallery in the Houses of Parliament on the morning of 3 January 2000 as part of the First Weekend Millennium celebrations. It was hosted on behalf of the Government by the Department for Culture, Media and Sport, (DCMS) and the opening welcome was given by its then Secretary of State, Rt Hon Chris Smith MP. It was held in the presence of Their Royal Highnesses the Duke and Duchess of Gloucester and was attended by the Prime Minister, the Home Secretary and the Speaker of the House of Commons together with faith community representatives and other distinguished guests.

Some 45 speakers and musicians from all parts of the UK took part in the programme of the event. Towards the end of it, leading faith community representatives invited the audience to join them in the Act of Commitment. The text of this (which has been used subsequently in a number of other events) is reproduced overleaf. The event ended with some concluding reflections from the Prime Minister.

An Act of Commitment

Faith community representatives:

In a world scarred by the evils of war, racism, injustice and poverty, we offer this joint Act of Commitment as we look to our shared future.

All:

We commit ourselves,
as people of many faiths,
to work together
for the common good,
uniting to build a better society,
grounded in values and ideals we share:

> community,
> personal integrity,
> a sense of right and wrong,
> learning, wisdom and love of truth,
>
> care and compassion,
> justice and peace,
> respect for one another,
> for the earth and its creatures.

We commit ourselves,
in a spirit of friendship and co-operation,
to work together
alongside all who share our values and ideals,
to help bring about a better world
now and for generations to come.

Resources

I ORGANISATIONS

a) UK and national inter faith organisations

The Inter Faith Network for the UK
8A Lower Grosvenor Place
London SW1W OEN
Tel: 020 7931 7766
Fax: 020 7931 7722
e-mail: ifnet@interfaith.org.uk
website: www.interfaith.org.uk

The Inter Faith Network was established in 1987 to foster good relations between different religious communities at both national and local level. It works with its member bodies to help make Britain a country marked by mutual understanding and respect between religions where all can practise their faith with integrity. The Network's way of working is firmly based on the principle that dialogue and co-operation can only prosper if they are rooted in respectful relationships which do not blur or undermine the distinctiveness of different religious traditions.

Its 111 member organisations include representative bodies of the Baha'i, Buddhist, Christian, Hindu, Jain, Jewish, Muslim, Sikh and Zoroastrian communities, as well as national and local inter faith organisations and educational bodies with an interest in inter faith issues. All member bodies of the Network subscribe to the document, *Building Good Relations with People of Different Faiths and Beliefs,* the text of which is reproduced at Annex B.

The Inter Faith Network's activities include:

- running an information service about faith communities and inter faith issues

- linking national and local inter faith initiatives in the UK and sharing good practice between them through meetings and publications, including its newsletter *Inter Faith Update*

- fostering local inter faith co-operation and offering advice on patterns of local inter faith initiatives suitable to the particular local area as well as helpful contacts

- holding national and regional meetings and events focusing on particular aspects of life in multi faith Britain

- publishing inter faith resource materials

A list of contact points for all the Network's member bodies can be obtained from the Network

Northern Ireland, Scotland and Wales

There are inter faith bodies in membership of the Inter Faith Network which handle inter faith relations in Northern Ireland, Scotland and Wales. These are best placed to help local inter faith initiatives in their areas. Their contact details are:

Scottish Inter Faith Council
St Francis' Centre
405 Cumberland Street
Glasgow G5 0SE
Scotland
Tel: 0141 429 4012
Email: admin@interfaithscotland.org
Website: www.interfaithscotland.org

Inter Faith Council for Wales
c/o 23 Solva Avenue
Llanishen
Cardiff CF14 0NP
Wales
Email: aschwartz@clara.co.uk

Northern Ireland Inter Faith Forum
c/o Stranmillis University College
Stranmillis Road
Belfast BT9 5DY
Northern Ireland
Email: interfaithni@stran.ac.uk

Other national inter faith organisations

The following inter faith organisations can assist local inter faith initiatives with advice and information relating to their particular focus within the work of building good inter faith relations.

Council of Christians and Jews
Aims: To promote good relations between Christian and Jewish communities through understanding; to counteract prejudice and discrimination, and to work together for a just society.

Council of Christians and Jews
1st Floor Camelford House
87-89 Albert Embankment
London SE1 7TP
Tel: 020 7820 0090
Email: cjrelations@ccj.org.uk
Website: www.ccj.org.uk

International Association for Religious Freedom (British Chapter)
Aims: to support the International Association for Religious Freedom in promotion of its aim of working for freedom of religion and belief at a global level.

International Association for Religious Freedom (British Chapter)
Upper Chapel
Norfolk Street
Sheffield S1 2JD
Tel: 0114 276 7114

Maimonides Foundation
Aims: To foster good relations and understanding, based on dialogue and mutual respect, between Jews and Muslims in this country and abroad.

Maimonides Foundation
Nour House
6 Hill Street
London W1J 5NF
Tel: 020 7518 8282
Email: info@maimonides-foundation.org
Website: www.maimonides-foundation.org

Religions for Peace (UK)

Aims: To transform conflict by peaceful means; promote human rights; protect orphans and other vulnerable children; support community development and ecology; increase security and disarmament; and advance peace education.

Religions for Peace (UK)
c/o London Inter Faith Centre
125 Salusbury Road
London NW6 6RG
Tel: 01962 774221
Email: hopeis@btinternet.com
Website: www.religionsforpeace.org.uk

Three Faiths Forum

Aims: To promote dialogue, friendship and understanding at all levels, but particularly at grassroots level, between Christians, Jews and Muslims.

Three Faiths Forum
Star House
104-108 Grafton Road
London NW5 4BA
Tel: 020 7485 2538
Email: threefaiths@sternberg-foundation.co.uk
Website: www.threefaithsforum.org.uk

United Religions Initiative (UK)

Aims: To promote enduring, daily inter faith co-operation; to end religiously-motivated violence; and to create cultures of peace, justice and healing for the Earth and all living beings.

United Religions Initiative (UK)
Northside
Grange in Borrowdale
Keswick
Cumbria CA19 5UQ
Tel: 01768 777671
Email: info@uri.org.uk
Website: www.uri.org.uk

World Congress of Faiths

Aims: To promote fellowship – ie a deep spiritual connection and friendship – between followers of all faiths; to revitalise individuals' spiritual being through religion and to encourage study of religions; to respect and celebrate the individual religious faiths of members.

World Congress of Faiths
125 Salusbury Road
London NW6 6RG
Tel: 020 8959 3129 or 01935 864055
Email: enquiries@worldfaiths.org
Website: www.worldfaiths.org

b) Regional and local inter faith organisations

A list of regional and local inter faith bodies around the UK with email contact details can be found on the Inter Faith Network's website www.interfaith.org.uk. More information about the work of these bodies can be found in *Inter Faith Organisations in the UK: A Directory* (see under Resources: Publications).

c) UK faith community organisations

The following are faith community umbrella or representative bodies in membership of the Inter Faith Network which will usually be able to respond both to enquiries about local places of worship of their tradition and to more general questions.

Baha'i
Baha'i Community of the United Kingdom
27 Rutland Gate
London SW7 1PD
Tel: 020 7584 2566
Email: nsa@bahai.org.uk
Website: www.bahai.org.uk

Buddhist
Network of Buddhist Organisations (UK)
6 Tyne Road
Bishopstone
Bristol BS7 8EE
Tel: 0117 924 8819
Email: interfaith@nbo.org.uk
Website: www.nbo.org.uk

Buddhist Society
58 Eccleston Square
London SW1V 1PH
Tel: 020 7834 5858
Email: info@thebuddhistsociety.org.uk
Website: info@thebuddhistsociety.org.uk

Christian
Churches Together in Britain and Ireland
Bastille Court
2 Paris Gardens
London SE1 8ND
Tel: 020 7654 7254
Email: info@ctbi.org.uk
Website: www.ctbi.org.uk

Hindu
Hindu Council (UK)
126-128 Uxbridge Road
London W13 8QS
Tel: 020 8566 5656
Email: office@hinducounciluk.org
Website: www.hinducounciluk.org

Hindu Forum of Britain
Unit 3, Vascroft Estate
861 Coronation Road
Park Royal
London NW10 7PT
Tel: 020 8965 0671
Email: info@hinduforum.org
Website: http://www.hinduforum.org

National Council of Hindu Temples
62 Oakdene Road
Watford WD24 6RW
Tel: 01923 350093
Email: bimal.krsna.bcs@pamho.net

Jain
Jain Samaj Europe
20 James Close
London NW11 9QX
Tel: 020 8455 5573
Email: natubhaishah@aol.com

Jewish
Board of Deputies of British Jews
6 Bloomsbury Square
London WC1A 2LP
Tel: 020 7543 5400
Email: info@bod.org.uk
Website: www.bod.org.uk

Muslim
Muslim Council of Britain
Boardman House
64 Broadway
Stratford
London E15 1NT
Tel: 020 8432 0585
Email: admin@mcb.org.uk
Website: www.mcb.org.uk

Imams and Mosques Council
20-22 Creffield Road
London W5 3RP
Tel: 020 8992 6636
Email: msraza@muslimcollege.ac.uk
Website: www.muslimcollege.ac.uk/pages/links/imams.html

Sikh
Network of Sikh Organisations (UK)
43 Dorset Road
Merton Park
London SW19 3EZ
Tel: 020 8544 8037
Email: nso@sikhismuk.fsnet.co.uk
Website: www.nsouk.co.uk

Zoroastrian
Zoroastrian Trust Funds of Europe
440 Alexandra Avenue
Harrow
Middlesex HA2 9TL
Tel: 020 8866 0765
Email: secretary@ztfe.com
Website: www.ztfe.com

For information on new religious movements

Information Network Focus on Religious Movements (INFORM) helps enquirers by giving them information directly or by putting them in touch with its extensive network of experts. Its research covers the collection, analysis and provision of information about the diverse beliefs and practices of New Religious Movements. It runs an information help line for enquirers.

Information Network Focus on Religious Movements
Houghton Street
London WC2A 2AE
Tel: 020 7955 7654
Email: inform@lse.ac.uk
Website: www.lse.ac.uk/collections/INFORM/

d) Government

The Inner Cities Religious Council

Inner Cities Religious Council (ICRC)
Neighbourhood Renewal Unit
Office of the Deputy Prime Minister
6/J2 Eland House
Bressenden Place
London SW1E 5DU
Tel: 020 7944 3704
Email: icrc@odpm.gsi.gov.uk
website: www.neighbourhood.gov.uk/page.asp?id=524

The Inner Cities Religious Council (ICRC) is a forum for members of faith communities to work with the Government on issues of regeneration, neighbourhood renewal, social inclusion, and other relevant cross-departmental policies and processes. The ICRC was established in 1992 and is chaired by a Government Minister from the Office of the Deputy Prime Minister (ODPM). It includes members from the five largest faith communities in urban areas in England: Christians; Hindus; Jews; Muslims and Sikhs. There are normally three ICRC meetings a year to discuss issues, policies and programmes. Members speak on behalf of their communities while other Ministers, officials and speakers – often from other Government departments – attend as appropriate. In this way the Council ensures that faith perspectives are heard throughout Government and beyond. Outside meetings members liaise with their communities and help promote action by faith communities to combat social exclusion and develop sustainable communities.

The ICRC Secretariat can provide: information on current regeneration programmes; names of ICRC members, if local groups wish ICRC members to bring their experience, positive or negative, to the attention of Ministers and officials; contacts with other local groups pioneering similar work with a regeneration dimension; addresses of local Regional Development Agency officials and officials from the Government Offices for the Regions; free publications such as conference reports.

There is no precise equivalent to the ICRC for Northern Ireland, Scotland or Wales.

Cohesion and Faiths Unit of the Home Office

Cohesion and Faiths Unit
Home Office
1st Floor, Seacole Building
2 Marsham Street
London
Tel: 0870 000 1585
Website: www.homeoffice.gov.uk

The Cohesion and Faiths Unit (CFU) is a new unit created in early 2005 from the merger of the former Community Cohesion Unit and Faith Communities Unit. CFU is part of the Race, Cohesion, Equality and Faith Directorate which is, in turn, part of the Communities Group. This works towards one of the Home Office's key objectives, which is that citizens, communities and the voluntary sector should be more fully engaged in tackling social problems and for there to be more equality of opportunity and respect for people of all races and religions.

The Government's strategy to increase race equality and community cohesion, set out in *Improving Opportunity, Strengthening Society,* and the recommendations of the Steering Group reviewing patterns of engagement between Government and faith communities in England, set out in Working Together: Cooperation between Government and Faith Communities, provide a framework for the Unit's work. This agenda affects the whole of central Government, necessitating work with, and through, other Government departments, local government bodies, non departmental public bodies, the voluntary and community sector, and faith groups. The Unit's work relates to the following linked themes:

- Creating a shared sense of belonging
- Tackling racism and extremism
- Supporting areas experiencing challenges to cohesion
- Engaging with, and building capacity in, faith communities.

e) *Other*

The Faith Based Regeneration Network UK (FbRN)

FbRN aims to encourage the active engagement of faith groups in local regeneration initiatives and partnerships; to build the skills of faith based regeneration practitioners and capacity of faith communities; and to demonstrate the benefit of cross-faith collaboration for the common good while respecting the diversity and plurality of traditions.

Faith-Based Regeneration Network UK
Suite J2
Fourth Floor, Charles House
375 Kensington High Street
London W14 8QH
Tel: 020 7471 6791/2
Email: admin@fbrn.org.uk
Website: www.fbrn.org.uk

II PUBLICATIONS

a) Selected publications relating to inter faith activity

Building Good Relations with People of Different Faiths and Beliefs. A short set of guidelines for inter faith encounter, developed by the member organisations of the Inter Faith Network. Published by the Inter Faith Network, 1993. Printed on at Annex B of this guide and can be downloaded from www.interfaith.org.uk

Connect: Different Faiths Shared Values. An inter faith action guide for young people. Published by the Inter Faith Network in assocation with the National Youth Agency and TimeBank, 2004. Available to download from www.interfaith.org.uk/connect

Inter Faith Update. Newsletter of the Inter Faith Network published three times a year. For details see the Network's website www.interfaith.org.uk

Inter Faith Organisations in the UK: A Directory. A directory listing details of over 200 organisations working to promote good inter faith relations at UK-wide, national, regional and local level. Second Edition. Published by the Inter Faith Network, 2005. Third edition due 2006.

Local Inter Faith Activity in the UK: A Survey. This report details the findings of a six month survey in 2003 which mapped the changing landscape of local inter faith activity around the UK. Published by theInter Faith Network, 2003. Available to download from: www.interfaith.org.uk/publications.htm

Mission, Dialogue and Inter Religious Encounter. Does true dialogue inevitably exclude mission? What are the ethics of mission and of dialogue in a multi faith country? This consultative document was issued by the Inter Faith Network in 1993 to encourage discussion and reflection on these issues.

Religions in the UK: A Directory, 2001-3, ed Paul Weller. Published by the Multi-Faith Centre, University of Derby in association with the Inter Faith Network, 2001. Contains listings of faith community national bodies, local places of worship and religious organisations, and inter faith organisations and chapters about the main faith communities of the UK, created with their assistance and chapters about: the religious landscape of the UK, inter faith activity in the UK, and a range of other issues involved in making contact with people of a faith other than one's own.

Shap Calendar of World Religious Festivals: A wall calendar and accompanying booklet giving details of the key festivals each year. For ordering details, contact the Shap Working Party, c/o The National RE Centre, 32 Causton Street, London, SW1P 4AU Tel: 020 7932 1194.

b) Selected publications relating to running small voluntary organisations

General

Just About Managing? Effective Management for Voluntary Organisations and Community Groups, Fourth Edition, Sandy Adirondack, London Voluntary Service Council, 2005.

Voluntary But Not Amateur: A Guide to the Law for Voluntary Organisations and Community Groups, Seventh Edition, Ruth Hayes and Jacki Reason, London Voluntary Service Council, 2004.

The Voluntary Sector Legal Handbook, Second Edition, Sandy Adirondack and James Sinclair Taylor, Directory of Social Change, 2001. New edition planned for 2006.

Funding

The Compact on Relations between Government and the Voluntary and Community Sector (and Codes of Good Practice on Consultation, Volunteering, Black and Minority Ethnic Sector and Community Organisations), Home Office, Communications Directorate, 1998 (and 2000-2004). For further information and to download: www.thecompact.org.uk

The Directory of Grant Making Trusts 2005-06, Directory of Social Change, in assocation with the Charities Aid Foundation, 2005.

The Funding and Procurement Compact Code of Good Practice. Home Office, 2005 (revised from the 2001 edition). For further information and to download: www.thecompact.org.uk

A Guide to Local Trusts, with volumes on Greater London, the Midlands, the North of of England the South of England. Published biannually by Directory of Social Change.

A Guide to the Major Trusts Volumes I and II, published biannually Directory of Social Change.

A Guide to Scottish Trusts, John Smyth. Published biannually by Directory of Social Change.

The Welsh Funding Guide, Alan French, John Smyth and Tom Traynor. Published biannually by Directory of Social Change.

Media

The DIY Guide to Public Relations, Moi Ali, Directory of Social Change, 1999.

Media Trust guidance at www.mediatrust.org

Working with young people

Safe from Harm: A Code of Practice for Safeguarding the Welfare of Children in Voluntary Organisations in England and Wales. With an introduction by Ministers from the Home Office, Department of Health, Department for Education and the Welsh Office, Home Office, London, 1993. Available to download at www.homeoffice.gov.uk/docs/harm.html. See also *Caring for Young People and the Vulnerable*, Home Office, 1999. Available to download from www.homeoffice.gov.uk/docs/young.pdf

StopCheck: A Step by Step Guide for Organisations to Safeguard Children. NSPCC, 2004. Can be downloaded at www.nspcc.org.uk/inform/downloads/Stopcheck.pdf

c) Selected publications relating to faith communities, inter faith issues and Government

Community Cohesion: An Action Guide, Local Government Association in partnership with the Home Office, the Office of the Deputy Prime Minister, the Audit Commission, the Commission for Racial Equality, the Improvement and Development Agency, and the Inter Faith Network, 2004.

Faith and Community: A Good Practice Guide for Local Authorities, Local Government Association in association with the Inner Cities Religious Council of the ODPM, the Active Community Unit of the Home Office, and the Inter Faith Network, 2002.

Focus on Religion, Office for National Statistics, 2004. Available to download from www.statistics.gov.uk/focuson/religion

Guidance on Community Cohesion, Local Government Association in association with the Home Office, Office of the Deputy Prime Minister, Commission for Racial Equality and the Inter Faith Network, 2002.

Improving Opportunity, Strengthening Society: the Government's Strategy to increase Race Equality and Community Cohesion, Home Office, 2005.

Partnership for the Common Good: Inter Faith Structures and Local Government, Inter Faith Network in association with the Home Office, the Office of the Deputy Prime Minister and the Local Government Association, 2003.

Working Together: Cooperation between Government and Faith Communities, Home Office, 2004

Note: Home Office documents can be downloaded from www.homeoffice.gov.uk and LGA publications from www.lga.gov.uk

Inter Faith Network for the UK
Member Organisations

Faith Community Representative Bodies

Arya Pratinidhi Sabha (UK)
Baha'i Community of the United Kingdom
Board of Deputies of British Jews
Buddhist Society
Churches Agency for Inter Faith Relations in Scotland
Churches' Commission for Inter-Faith Relations (Churches Together in Britain and Ireland)
Council of African and Afro-Caribbean Churches (UK)
Friends of the Western Buddhist Order
Hindu Council (UK)
Hindu Forum of Britain
Imams and Mosques Council (UK)
Islamic Cultural Centre, Regents Park, London
Jain Samaj Europe
Jamiat-e-Ulama Britain (Association of Muslim Scholars)
Muslim Council of Britain
National Council of Hindu Temples
Network of Buddhist Organisations (UK)
Network of Sikh Organisations (UK)
Quaker Committee for Christian and Interfaith Relations
Roman Catholic Committee for Other Faiths, Bishops' Conference of England and Wales
Sri Lankan Sangha Sabha of GB
Swaminarayan Hindu Mission
Unitarian and Free Christian Churches Interfaith Subcommittee
Vishwa Hindu Parishad (UK)
World Ahlul-Bayt Islamic League
World Islamic Mission (UK)
Zoroastrian Trust Funds of Europe

Inter Faith Organisations

Northern Ireland Inter Faith Forum
Scottish Inter Faith Council
Inter Faith Council for Wales/ Cyngor Cyd-Ffydd Cymru
Alif Aleph UK
Christians Aware Interfaith Programme

Council of Christians and Jews
Interfaith Foundation
International Association for Religious Freedom (British Chapter)
International Interfaith Centre
London Society of Jews and Christians
Maimonides Foundation
Minorities of Europe Inter Faith Action Programme
Religions for Peace (UK Chapter)
Three Faiths Forum
United Religions Initiative (Britain and Ireland)
Westminster Interfaith
World Congress of Faiths

Local Inter Faith Groups

Altrincham Inter Faith Group
Bedford Council of Faiths
Birmingham Council of Faiths
Blackburn with Darwen Interfaith Council
Bolton Interfaith Council
Bradford Concord Interfaith Society
Brent Inter Faith
Brighton and Hove Inter-Faith Contact Group
Bristol Inter Faith Group
Burnley Building Bridges
Cambridge Inter-Faith Group
Canterbury and District Inter Faith Action
Cardiff Interfaith Association
Cleveland Interfaith Group
Coventry Inter Faith Group
Coventry Multi Faith Forum
Derby Open Centre Multi-Faith Group
Dudley Borough Interfaith Network
Gateshead Inter Faith Forum
Gloucestershire Inter Faith Action
Harrow Inter Faith Council
Hounslow Friends of Faith
Huddersfield Interfaith Council
Lancashire Forum of Faiths
Leeds Concord Interfaith Fellowship
Leeds Faith Communities Liaison Forum
Leicester Council of Faiths
Loughborough Council of Faiths
Luton Council of Faiths
Manchester Interfaith Forum
Medway Inter Faith Action
Merseyside Council of Faiths

Interfaith MK (Milton Keynes)
Nelson and Brierfield Building Bridges
Newcastle Council of Faiths
Newham Faith Sector Forum
North Kirklees Inter-Faith Council
North Staffordshire Forum of Faiths
Northampton Faiths Forum
Nottingham Inter Faith Council
Oldham Inter Faith Forum
Oxford Round Table of Religions
Peterborough Inter-Faith Council
Reading Inter-Faith Group
Redbridge Council of Faiths
Rochdale Multifaith Partnership
Sheffield Interfaith
South London Inter Faith Group
Southampton Council of Faiths
Suffolk Inter-Faith Resource
Telford and Wrekin Interfaith Group
Warrington Council of Faiths
Watford Inter Faith Association
Wellingborough Multi-Faith Group
Whalley Range (Manchester) Inter Faith Group
Wolverhampton Inter-Faith Group
Wycombe Sharing of Faiths

Educational and Academic Bodies

Centre for the Study of Jewish-Christian Relations
Centre for the Study of Islam and Christian-Muslim Relations
Community Religions Project, University of Leeds
Institute of Jainology
Islamic Foundation
Multi-Faith Centre at the University of Derby
National Association of SACREs
Religious Education Council for England and Wales
Shap Working Party on World Religions in Education
Sion Centre for Dialogue and Encounter